portfolio" can literally change the world (and us!) as God transforms it into an "Eternity Portfolio."

Dave Ramsey
Best-selling author and nationally syndicated radio host of
The Dave Ramsey Show

There is a responsibility that comes with financial blessings. And, since it all belongs to God, we should be looking for how He would have us manage it. *The Eternity Portfolio* is a well thought out plan for making the most of your finances. I believe it will help my family, along with many others, grow to new levels of faithfulness.

Coach Mark Richt
Head coach, University of Georgia Football

I wish every Christian had an Eternity Portfolio! Alan Gotthardt's solidly biblical approach gives you a step-by-step guide to making financial and giving decisions with eternal rewards in mind. Follow the principles of this book and be blessed!

Luis Palau
International evangelist

While laying a solid biblical foundation for why we should give, this is a great "how to" book that shows how to formulate a true action plan for "laying up treasures in heaven" for eternity.

Hugh O. Maclellan, Jr.
Chairman, The Maclellan Foundation

Alan has delivered a compelling vision for investing in eternity that will reshape the way you think about your financial future. *The Eternity Portfolio* is fundamental truth that is powerful yet practical. I believe these principles will make a tremendous difference for all eternity as we focus our investing in God's strategic Kingdom work.

Josh McDowell
Best-selling author of **More Than a Carpenter**

As a church pastor for many years, I have used numerous books on stewardship and money management to instruct our people. But I do believe this is the most comprehensive and thorough work I have read. Alan has provided an extremely valuable resource for the church in this excellent work.

Randy Pope
Pastor, Perimeter Church

The Eternity Portfolio is a critical book. I know of no other like it. My husband and I are filled with excitement at the prospects of God multiplying and using our resources in an even more strategic way for the furtherance of His kingdom. What could be more important? I recommend this book for every child of God, rich or poor.

Kay Arthur
Best-selling author and president, Precept Ministries International

In a time when opportunities for excellent giving are increasing exponentially, we need to become far more *intentional* and *thoughtful* regarding how we steward what God has entrusted to us. *The Eternity Portfolio* book will be a key resource as you seek to make a difference, both now and for eternity. I highly commend it.

David Wills
President, National Christian Foundation

One of the reasons God has blessed America is in order to fund the Great Commission. Alan Gotthardt has delivered a book full of compelling and practical strategies for how each Christian can have a financial stake in that plan. *The Eternity Portfolio* is a must-read for those who want to experience the excitement and joy that comes from investing in eternity. Don't miss out on this opportunity of a lifetime.

Larry Burkett
Founder, Crown Financial Ministries

When it comes to stewardship, Alan Gotthardt is on the cutting edge. *The Eternity Portfolio* has challenged and encouraged me and has confirmed how God is leading our family to be intentional about investing in eternity. This book is a "must-read" for anyone serious about their faith and their money.

Dr. Johnny M. Hunt
Senior pastor, First Baptist Church Woodstock

Alan Gotthardt's book, *The Eternity Portfolio*, is going to make a major and positive difference in the way and the places you invest. You are going to be a whole lot more effective at it and a whole lot more pleased when you do it. Money isn't, you see, only about how you get it, it's about what you do with it. This is a book that will make a major and positive difference in your life and for the kingdom of God.

Steve Brown
Founder, Key Life Network

Books on stewardship and giving abound, but are seldom very original or particularly helpful. Alan Gotthardt's *The Eternity Portfolio* is the first book I have seen that actually covers new ground by telling a believer how to maximize his investment and consequently his giving to kingdom causes. I pray that every church will gain access to this excellent work.

Dr. Paige Patterson
President, Southwestern Baptist Theological Seminary

For most people, when it comes to faithfully handling money, giving is the final frontier. Alan combines biblical wisdom with financial strategy to create a solid plan for your giving that will change your life. It is a great book. After you read *The Eternity Portfolio*, your vision for long-term investing will never be the same.

Howard Dayton
CEO, Compass, author of **Your Money Counts**

Alan Gotthardt connects the dots in one of the most critical areas of our lives. With a total paradigm shift on creating wealth and investing with purpose, this highly devotional book is a must-read. If every church member reads and acts on this practical wisdom, our churches will never again need to beg for money and will soar in their endeavors for the kingdom.

Jay H. Strack
President, Student Leadership University

Alan Gotthardt's book has coined a phrase that I hope churches in the future will use over and over: *The Eternity Portfolio.* His sound, biblically based insights keep us focused on truly long-term investments that build up the kingdom of God.

Dr. Bryant Wright
Senior pastor, Johnson Ferry Baptist Church

Alan Gotthardt delivers a convincing explanation of Jesus' teaching that it is in a Christian's enlightened self-interest to be generous. Gotthardt systematically shows how to be a wise and effective investor in God's kingdom by following biblical principles. If the people of America who call ourselves "Christian" were to truly believe God's promises about money and follow His principles of wise giving, countless lives would be changed for Christ around the world.

Laurence Powell
President, Powell Family Enterprises

THE ETERNITY PORTFOLIO

PORTFOLIO

ILLUMINATED

∞

ALAN GOTTHARDT

THE ETERNITY PORTFOLIO

PORTFOLIO

ILLUMINATED

ALAN GOTTHARDT

Deep River
BOOKS

Edited by Karin Stock Buursma, Annette LaPlaca, Michael Degan
Interior design: Robin Black, Inspirio Design
Cover design: Jason Enterline

ISBN: 9781940269658

Library of Congress: 2015910802

Published by Deep River Books
Sisters, Oregon 97759

Printed in the United States of America

CONTENTS

Foreword. 13

Preface. 15

Acknowledgments. 17

Introduction: A Tale of Three Managers. 19

Chapter 1 29
Faithful Managers: Investing with Their Values

Chapter 2 41
The Ultimate Investment

Chapter 3 61
The Eternity Portfolio

Chapter 4 79
Funding the Portfolio: How Much Is Enough for Now?

Chapter 5 111
Funding the Portfolio: How Much Is Enough for Good?

Chapter 6 129
God's Asset Allocation

Chapter 7 155
Making Wise Investments

Chapter 8 189
Passing the Baton: A Legacy That Outlasts You

Chapter 9 211
The Seven Golden Keys to Investing for Eternity

Appendix A Case Studies 225

Appendix B Eternity Portfolio Policy Statement. 241

Appendix C Due Diligence Checklist 249

Appendix D Resources 253

Appendix E Historical Quotes on Eternal Rewards 257

About the Author and Guest Contributors. 263

Notes. 269

FOREWORD

What would happen if we saw giving as a way of investing? If we gave our giving "portfolio" the same attention we give our retirement portfolio? What would happen if we stopped asking, "How much do I have to give?" and started asking, "How can I invest in eternity by giving?" How would our lives change if we became aware of the rewards of faithfully investing our resources? Alan Gotthardt asks these questions, and his answer is *The Eternity Portfolio*.

There are many books on the market about the principles of managing money and many books about why Christians should give. But Alan's thought-provoking book is unique because it combines the two concepts and takes them to the next level by including the family and ministry in the plan. In an approach that's grounded in Scripture, Alan leads you through the process of how to fund, design, implement, and monitor your Eternity Portfolio. He takes his expertise as a financial planner and applies it to the idea of radical generosity.

Alan communicates a compelling vision for the kingdom of God as the ultimate long-term investment, and he gives a step-by-step plan for how you can have a part in this incredible opportunity. With charts, graphs, income-tax and estate-planning information, detailed case studies, and reflective questions, this book is extremely practical. It provides what you need to start maximizing your investment in the kingdom of God. The tools to succeed are in your hands!

As Christians in America, we are living in a time of unprecedented wealth and luxury, yet many Christians give a smaller percentage of their income now than at any other time in history. Alan makes the case that we are missing God's perspective on investing for the long-term. The powerful message of *The Eternity Portfolio* can change lives. Think of the huge impact on ministry across the world if Christians began to invest generously for eternity!

I encourage you to read this book. Your life and your view of eternity will never be the same.

John C. Maxwell
Bestselling author of *The 21 Irrefutable Laws of Leadership*

PREFACE

The *Eternity Portfolio* was first published in the fall of 2003. It got caught up in—and, I hope, contributed to—the wave of intentional, Christian generosity that really began rising in the 1990s and has reached epic proportions since. Never before in history have so many Christians—rich and poor—been focused on stewarding their material possessions in light of Christ's eternal kingdom. God has blessed the message of intentional generosity, and I've been privileged to hear the stories of how *The Eternity Portfolio* has impacted so many around the world.

For many years now, in writing and speaking across North America, I've addressed questions from those who earnestly desire God's best for their finances—questions about integrating their Family Portfolio and their Eternity Portfolio, questions about eternal rewards and godly motives, questions about business thinking and entrepreneurship in light of eternity, questions about how to give more effectively, and so on. This new edition may bring clarity to persistent questions while at the same time communicating the nuance that keeps us asking our Father for ongoing direction. Also, inspired by several of my hedge fund heroes who wrote *The Most Important Thing*,[1] I invited a number of incredibly talented and experienced givers to add their insights to the work. They played a big role in *illuminating* this edition, and I know you will appreciate their commentary throughout.

After extensive review—by myself and others—I have preserved the original work as the core of this expanded volume. The scriptural framework is timeless, and the concepts continue to chart a strategic path for those who want to manage their finances intentionally in light of eternity. Additions and guest comments provide a major enhancement, and we've highlighted the additions with the symbol 💡.

Finally, I'd like to dedicate this Illuminated edition to my pastor, Dr. Johnny Hunt, and my business partner, David McKinnon. Without them, the trajectory of my story would have been very different. Their lives of generosity—financial and relational—are the greatest I've had the privilege of knowing.

Alan Gotthardt
February 2015

ACKNOWLEDGMENTS

The global community of generous givers has been a huge source of wisdom, encouragement, and inspiration on my journey, and I'm grateful for organizations like Generous Giving, the National Christian Foundation, and others for bringing so many of us together. Then, a big thank you to David Wills, Todd Harper, Heather Tuininga, Larry Powell, Jack Alexander, Lorne Jackson, and Dr. Johnny Hunt for their review, challenging questions, and guest commentary throughout this new edition. Special thanks to Sharon Epps for insightful help shaping the segment on giving as a couple, and to Charlie Jordan for assistance on the case studies. The wisdom of these experienced givers makes this edition broader and deeper as we look to empower a new generation of kingdom investors.

This book would not have been possible without the lifelong training and example of my parents, Fred and Gladys Gotthardt. To them I say, "Thank you, and know that as God has used *The Eternity Portfolio*, it is a return on your investment in me." Finally, in our twenty-fifth year of marriage, I'm indebted to my wife, Melissa, a treasure God gave before I could appreciate even a small part of its worth. She and I frequently comprise the joint subject when *I/me* or *we/our* is referenced in the book. This story is truly our story. Melissa's role and calling, although very different from mine, are a delightful, essential element of our life's work together.

INTRODUCTION

A TALE OF THREE MANAGERS

There once was a wealthy man who was departing on a long journey. He planned to be gone for an indefinite period of time—maybe a few years, maybe even a few decades. In preparation for this extended absence, he called his three trusted financial managers and divided his assets among them.

"Take this money and use it to further my interests," he charged each one.

The wise owner knew the abilities of each of the managers and divided the funds accordingly. To Charlie Wise he gave $5 million, to Sarah Prudence $2 million, and to Jeffrey Short $1 million.

Confident that his affairs were in order, the owner set sail, not to be seen again for many years. Charlie and Sarah set to work immediately, laying plans for several investment ventures. Charlie had this great idea the owner had given him about starting franchise operations of the owner's business. The owner's product was such that it really sold itself. Those who had a need for it just kept coming, and they couldn't help but introduce it to their friends and acquaintances. Charlie communicated daily with the owner via phone and e-mail. Over the years Charlie partnered with others affiliated with the owner to establish a worldwide distribution network for the product. Business was booming and the profits were really starting to accelerate when the owner returned.

Sarah spent a good deal of time studying written instructions the wealthy owner had left behind. After communicating with him on some initial strategic issues, she felt confident of the right direction for her investment. Sarah developed a marketing division for the owner's main product line that gave away free samples and promoted goodwill and interest in the owner. Sarah was in constant communication with him and was able to market his true persona effectively. Sales began to flow, and although Sarah's division did not see all the results directly, she knew from the company field reports that she was having a huge impact. It seemed like they were just getting started when the owner returned.

Jeffrey was really excited at the prospect of $1 million. *Look what the owner gave me!* he thought. *The world is at my disposal.* He seemed to recall some vague instruction about the owner's interest, but Jeffrey was not much for communication, and he didn't have time to read any of the owner's written instructions. *If he is going away for such a long time, I need to earn a living,* he thought. *Who knows when or even if the owner will return?* Jeffrey set aside most of the money in a safe-deposit box at the bank. He used some to start a personal business and became successful in his own right. Every now and then, someone would mention to him his responsibility as a manager of the owner's money. Out of guilt, he would return a little of what he was using to the safe-deposit box. He figured that in a few more years there would be opportunity to focus on the owner's investment. But time passed quickly, and fear struck Jeffrey's heart when he heard the owner had returned.

The owner called in the managers to give account for their service. "I am so glad to see you," he began. "I really trusted you when I gave you my fortune to invest, and I can't wait to see how you've done."

Charlie could hardly contain his excitement. "At first I wasn't sure how your big idea would ever be successful, but the more we talked and the further things went, the more I bought in to the whole strategy." He handed over a bank statement that showed $10 million in the corporate account. "And that's just the profits we have collected," Charlie said, beaming. "It's difficult to measure the value of the whole empire!"

The owner was obviously pleased. "Well done, my friend. You have managed my investment faithfully for all these years. You could have enjoyed a lot of smaller pleasures along the way, but I think you'll be pleased with what is in store for you." The owner explained the new and greater responsibilities he had for Charlie and the enormous reward set aside for his faithfulness.

Charlie was almost speechless in his joy and gratitude, but he managed to stammer, "It seems like so much for the effort I expended . . . with *your* money."

Seeing Charlie leave the owner's office with a dazed smile on his face, Sarah was a little apprehensive. She quietly handed over the financial statements for her division, with $4 million showing on the balance sheet. "It seems somewhat small after all these years," Sarah began, but the owner interrupted her with a wave of his hand.

"On the contrary, Sarah, you have done well. This is a good return on my investment, and yet you don't know a fraction of what has accrued to my empire as a result of your diligent efforts." Sarah was thrilled as the owner explained the vast treasure that was hers, along with a new and greater role in the company's management. "All those sacrifices along the way were duly noted, Sarah," he said. "The hours you put in, the financial commitment— none were forgotten. You made the most of my investment."

Sarah couldn't help but wonder at the seeming inequity of the whole thing. "I only did what I was instructed . . . And in return, all this?"

Upon hearing of the owner's return, Jeffrey had scrambled to pull together the $1 million the owner had entrusted to his care. It seemed so small after all these years that he had the bank give it to him in bags of fives and tens so it would look more significant. As he approached the owner, the excuses began. "Here it is, all $1 million. I knew you were a ruthless owner, and it scared me a little. So I kept your money safe in the bank, and now you can have it back."

The owner was extremely displeased to see no return on his money after so many years. "What do you mean, Jeffrey? You wicked and lazy manager!" he exclaimed. "You thought I was a ruthless owner, and yet you did *nothing* to make my money grow? Even if you had deposited it in a bank account, I would have earned something. I had great things planned for you. But you forfeited it all for the paltry returns of your own investments." The owner motioned to his guards. "Take the money from him and give it to Charlie Wise. And throw this worthless manager out on the street. He will never work again, and he will suffer loss forever for his mismanagement of my assets."

LIVING ON PURPOSE

Thus ends the extraordinary tale of the three managers—updated with creative license from the parable of the talents told by Jesus in Matthew 25:14–30. This parable represents the distilled essence of what the Bible says about our lives as managers of God's resources:

- We have been entrusted with money and material possessions.
- We should be intentional about God's plan for investing them.

- We will have to give an account for our management.
- We will be rewarded or suffer loss based on our faithfulness (or lack thereof).

Most people travel through life passively reacting to their surroundings and influences. Life just happens. Someone once said that 80 percent of success is merely showing up, and people tend to live in that fashion, giving little thought to the big picture. The Christian life, however, is meant to be lived *on purpose*. God has created us to live to His glory, and He has given us guidelines in the Bible for how that should work.

> Focusing on "purpose" is a key component to being an intentional investor. A family who agrees on their purpose lives in a purposeful way.
>
> *David Wills*

The apostle Paul writes that the true believer has died to himself and now lives *only* for the glory of God. This is a lofty standard, but if it's true, we who claim to be Christians must look for the direction God has for every aspect of our lives! Without vision and disciplined planning, we will miss out on the incredible joy, peace, and blessing that come to those who fully integrate their faith and life.

The backbone of that integration lies in the area of managing our material resources. We spend most of our waking hours earning, spending, saving, maintaining, and worrying about our possessions. Because this is a primary focus of our lives, those who want to be faithful managers must seek guidance in the only standard of truth we have—the Bible. Jesus was talking about the proper use of wealth in the book of Luke when He said:

> Whoever can be trusted with very little can also be trusted with much, and whoever is dishonest with very little will also be dishonest with much. So if you have not been trustworthy in

handling worldly wealth, who will trust you with true riches?
(Luke 16:10-11, NIV)

As we relinquish the practical matter of finances to God's direction, we begin to experience the abundance He wants for each part of our lives—both in our relationships with Him and with people. As we master the basics of faithful life management, our vision broadens. The more we understand God's priorities for His resources and what true riches are, the more we realize that when we give, we are *investing*—for His glory and our eternal reward.

> The Lord has made a deposit in my life. If I rightly invest His investment in me, there can be significant investment that will rebound to His glory. Question: What will I do with His investment in me?
>
> *Dr. Johnny Hunt*

This book was written to inspire your own vision for those eternal rewards and to equip you with a comprehensive strategy for making investments that last forever. Once you glimpse the future, however, there is no turning back. Since God opened my eyes to this reality, it has consumed my thinking and priorities. I have felt compelled to implement it in my own life. If you are like me, the concept of eternal rewards will be the most profound truth you will ever learn about using money.

> Some have a hard time equating giving with investing. After all, the traditional purpose for investing is to gain resources not give resources. At most, we might invest to gain so we can give more, right? Right.
>
> To see giving as a way of investing, back up one step and consider stewardship in general. Would Jesus use a story
>
> Continued on next page

about investing to paint a picture of stewardship? That's exactly what He does in the parable of the talents.

Generosity is the overarching theme of God's existence, His relationship with His creation, the reconciliation and restoration of it, and our daily response to it. Stewardship is the act of managing all that is entrusted to our care—both for ourselves and for those we are allowed to influence.

David Wills

The Eternity Portfolio is about *financial investing*. Although there are other parts of your life you can invest, such as your time and abilities, this book is about money. It is about the opportunity to commit your finances to something so big, so incredible, you will wonder how you could have missed it until now.

The Eternity Portfolio is about *maximum-growth investing*. The strategy outlined within these pages will generate returns far above anything you ever will achieve in your brokerage account, 401(k), IRA, or personal business.

The Eternity Portfolio is about *really long-term investing*. In the world of investments, *long-term* typically means greater than five years. For individuals, an investment horizon longer than thirty to forty years is unusual. The investment discussed in this book lasts much longer. In fact, this strategy will provide for your needs starting now and *literally* reaching to eternity.

The Eternity Portfolio is about *guaranteed investing*. An investment is only as good as the underlying asset or guarantor. For example, if you purchase a bond, that investment is only good if the issuing company is able to repay it with interest. The plan outlined in these pages is backed by the strongest guarantor with the best and longest credit rating in history. And unlike what we sometimes experience in our personal investments, the wealth of this guarantor is unaffected by stock-market fluctuations.

The strategy of *The Eternity Portfolio* will change the way you think about money—and it will change your life.

FOR A SPECIFIC AUDIENCE
WITH A SPECIAL PURPOSE

Over the last decade or so of teaching on generosity, one of the most common first responses I've heard on the topic is, "Well, you know, generosity isn't just about money." While true, the response comes so quickly—almost as a reflex—that it makes me wonder if the idea of "money generosity" hits a little too close to home. Interestingly, I've only heard this response from North American Christians, most of whom are doing just fine financially and all of whom are certainly among the richest Christians, both today and over the past 2000 years. And I'm not talking about the super-wealthy. In 2015, with $32,000 in annual income, you are in the top 1 percent of the world.[1] For this demographic, and assuming God uses money at all in His plan for redemption, it would seem that the first response should be, "Wow, God has entrusted more financial resources to me than most of the people who have ever lived. Beyond my time and talent, I want to be very intentional about shepherding this money." If that's what you're thinking, this book is for you.

I've also observed a wonderful revival of volunteerism, community service, and seeking social justice. Giving of the "personal self" has taken on new meaning and garnered major social status along the way. The world benefits as more of us engage with a spirit to do good—and God is pleased as we serve others. It has been said that giving of ourselves, particularly our precious time, is the most valuable gift. But reflecting on how we *actually use* so much of our time, it's not clear that we do value it so highly—except perhaps when using it as an alternative to financial generosity? It raises further questions: Valuable to whom? and, In what capacity? For example, if I take an hour out

Continued on next page

of each morning and paint my neighbor's mailbox—is that really serving him generously? Maybe, but how would I know? And is it possible after the third or fourth morning, the exercise is really more about me? Truly understanding where, how, and *even if* we are adding value in our personal service is a question we would be wise to ask regularly. I may benefit personally from almost any form of service, but isn't *value to the recipient* part of what makes it generosity versus just meeting my need to do good? I sometimes worry that despite good intentions, a strain of modern narcissism is creeping in, leading us at times to think more highly of our service than we ought, possibly even drowning out the voice of God, who wants to engage us at a deeper level.

Deeper perspectives on money—the most universal, albeit imperfect, standard of value and major driver of all activity in western culture—lie at the heart of going further up and further in. If you want to take that journey, this book is for you.

Then, I think about God's calling for each of us to play out our lives on a particular stage—using our unique abilities and emotional wiring for His glory. That might mean fighting for justice in the political system or serving soup in a homeless shelter, pastoring a church, leading a company, or creating works of art. It may mean fighting fires or working in an office or digging wells in Africa. *All the business of the kingdom. All creative, productive, helpful activities mirroring in some small way the majesty of our God.* But we can't do it all, and those committed to healthy lives—physical, spiritual, and relational—quickly realize the wisdom of Paul's teaching in 1 Corinthians 12 about the body of Christ. We are designed and brought together for different roles, not everyone doing a little of everything. This is cause for celebration in diversity, not guilt that we can't serve in every capacity. For those of us who get to choose what we do in life, it is cause for ongoing prayer for God's leading about how we can best serve. We seek His guidance, the wisdom of others, and self-awareness. For example, without very specific handwriting on the wall, I wouldn't feel called to serve as a caregiver in an Alzheimer's clinic. It's not a natural match for my gifts or how God has led me to this point. I probably wouldn't be very effective and might even be taking a spot on that stage that prevents a more suitable candidate from stepping up. Sometimes God calls us to areas way outside our abilities, but not often.

Not everyone gets to choose their path, particularly at different times in history (and in many parts of the world today), but for those who do, the consequences matter. If I abdicate the stage God has called me to—in my case as a business leader and investor—something goes lacking. Maybe it's providing jobs to people so they can feed their families or creating a specific product that is needed in the world. And whether we're artists or investors, truck drivers or pastors, the common thread of money runs through our business in the kingdom. And it's not just money, *but excess*, when considered in light of Paul's admonition that "if we have food and clothing" we should be content (1 Timothy 6:8). What should we do with the extra? Save it? Spend it? Reinvest it? Or give it away? Those who want to "seek first the kingdom of God" will wrestle with these questions. This book is for you.

Faithful Managers: Investing with Their Values

■ The truth about investing
■ How the faithful manager invests
■ God's two purposes for money
■ The investing equation

THE TRUTH ABOUT INVESTING

People often miss the point of investing money. After years of working with some of the wealthiest people in the world as an investor and advisor, I have encountered several common misconceptions. Some think of investing as a game to be won. Others see it as a goal in and of itself—to "be a successful investor." Most think of investing as a way to accumulate as much money as possible during their lifetime. Then there are a few who understand the real but hidden truth about investing—*it is a means to an end.*

Investing money is the process of committing resources in a strategic way to accomplish a specific objective. Done properly, investing will take you from where you are to where you want to go. In financial planning we think of investing in terms of a person's overall financial strategy (see chart). For optimal results, each part of your financial situation should be considered in light of the whole. Investing is simply a component of the financial strategy you must integrate with your entire plan.

Years ago I designed a portfolio for a newly widowed client in a unique situation. Most of Mrs. Brown's assets were in a trust that paid her the income generated each

STRATEGIC WEALTH MANAGEMENT

year. Since her husband's pension covered her modest living expenses, Mrs. Brown wanted to give away all of the income generated from the trust assets. Not only that, she wanted to *maximize* the income generated each year to be able to give away as much as possible during her lifetime. Most people in a similar situation would want to *minimize* the current income and maximize the long-term growth of the trust for the benefit of children or grandchildren many years down the road. Needless to say, the portfolio we developed for Mrs. Brown was very different from what we would typically use. Success for her was measured in a radically different way. Her life plan guided the strategy and made an impact on how she would invest her finances.

INVESTING BEGINS WITH VALUES

Money has no intrinsic value, only relative value. Its worth is measured by the ability to exchange it for something of value to the owner. In this light, the man who has no money and no wants is in the same position as one who has all the money in the world but cannot buy what he wants. In both cases, money is irrelevant because it cannot accomplish its purpose.

The point? *Investing is important as a means of accumulating money to be exchanged for something of value to you.*

Personal core values influence everything you do, and they should be the starting point for any investment plan. Your values represent who you are and what you consider important. Many influences shape and mold your core values, including family, friends, faith, and life experiences. These values define your life and should also be the basis for managing your finances. Your investment strategy will be truly effective only to the extent that it furthers your core values.

INVESTING IS ONLY MEANINGFUL IN TERMS OF YOUR VISION

Successful investing requires vision. You must be able to see at least a glimmer of the future rewards to understand that delayed gratification is worthwhile— that what is not spent on yourself today will be even more valuable in the years to come. When it comes to investing, vision is what turns a big spender into a big saver as retirement approaches. Vision enables a young couple to buy less and "eat in" more while putting aside funds for their child's college education. Vision motivates a person to give up *now* for the *future*. In a society constantly telling us to spend and consume at a frantic pace, vision enables us to ignore the siren song of instant gratification and instead focus on the future.

But a vision of what? Rewards. What type of rewards? *Those that are attractive based on your values.* Values are transformed to vision as you begin to see the potential reward. Your vision encompasses the goals and objectives you have for living your core values, and it understands the payoff—the reward for achieving your objectives.

For example, love for family is one of my core values. I want to be around my children, be a positive influence on them, and do everything possible to ensure their well-being. Each day I grow in my understanding of what it takes to live out that core value. I have a clearer vision of the objectives I must meet to accomplish that. From a relational standpoint, these might include eating dinner with my family each night of the week or reading Bible stories after dinner. From a financial standpoint, these include such things as providing housing, food, and clothing. Saving for college educations and for retirement are also parts of the long-term vision. And I picture the rewards, such as a happy and successful family and the personal benefits of good relationships. *Expectation of rewards brings vision for achieving them.*

INVESTING IS A STRATEGIC PROCESS

As you become passionate about your vision, you develop the discipline for achieving it. As a person pursues the reward, he will make hard choices and sacrifices. Discipline is the vehicle that drives a vision to fulfillment. For example, when you're saving for retirement, discipline forces you to consider spending patterns and invest a certain amount each month. Discipline requires a wise investment strategy focused on your long-term goals. It pushes you to monitor your plan and make adjustments where needed. Discipline creates and sustains a good investment strategy. Shown as an equation, investing might look something like this:

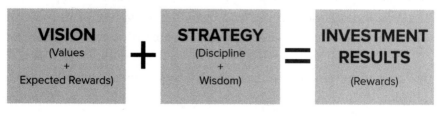

Let's start with the core value of loving my family. Over the years my **vision** increases and I understand more about what it means to love them—in this example, by providing financially. As the **rewards** become clear, my desire to achieve the goal expands my vision. That vision brings with it the **discipline** to create, implement, and monitor a **wise** financial **strategy** for making it all happen.

Whether the objective is retirement, a new car, or a college education, this equation holds true. When it comes to investing, the *clarity* of your vision and the *quality* of your strategy determine the degree of your success. We'll come back to this equation throughout the book to help us remember the factors that add up to investment results.

HOW THE FAITHFUL MANAGER INVESTS

What does this mean for the Christian who desires to be a faithful manager of the resources God provides? The details will vary from person to person, but there are common principles that form the foundation of an investment plan. The faithful manager wants to invest money with a clear vision and a quality strategy based on personal *values*. Equally important is the desire for the *rewards* of faithful management. Let's look at values, the first building block.

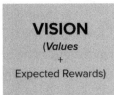

VISION
(Values
+
Expected Rewards)

In talking to Christians over the years, I have found that faithful managers share a set of core beliefs related to their stewardship responsibilities:

1. God owns everything and controls the distribution of wealth.
In Psalm 24:1 we read, "The earth is the Lord's, and all its fullness, the world and those who dwell therein." God created everything, and it all belongs to Him. He controls what happens to it. "Both riches and honor come from You, and You reign over all. In Your hand is power and might; in Your hand it is to make great and to give strength to all" (1 Chronicles 29:12).

A logical extension of this understanding is that God is in charge of providing everything we need. "Therefore do not worry, saying, 'What shall we eat?' or 'What shall we drink?' or 'What shall we wear?' . . . For your heavenly Father knows that you need all these things. But seek first the kingdom of God and His righteousness, and all these things shall be added to you" (Matthew 6:31–33). In his commentary on these verses, Dr. John MacArthur discusses the contrast between people of faith and those who have no hope:

> Those who have no hope in God naturally put their hope and expectations in things they can enjoy now. They have nothing to live for but the present, and their materialism is perfectly consistent with their religion. They have no God to supply their physical or their spiritual needs, their present or their eternal needs, so anything they get they must get for themselves. They are ignorant of God's supply and have no claim on it. No heavenly Father cares for them, so there is reason to worry.[1]

How different should our outlook as Christians be? Although we are to be obedient and work diligently, we know God is ultimately in control of all the financial resources that come our way.

2. We must all give an account of our stewardship.

Ecclesiastes 12:14 tells us that "God will bring every work into judgment, including every secret thing, whether good or evil." We know that God grants salvation and eternal life based on our faith in Jesus Christ. However, He will judge the works we do in His service on their merits and reward us accordingly. "For we must all appear before the judgment seat of Christ, that each one may receive the things done in the body, according to what he has done, whether good or bad" (2 Corinthians 5:10).

In this passage, Paul talks about a "judgment seat" similar to a legal bench in a modern-day courtroom. The one major difference will be the judge. Unlike an earthly judge, the One to whom we must give account already knows everything we have or haven't done, and He will judge our motives as well as our actions. Maybe this is why when the reformer Martin Luther thought about the judgment, he said that there were only two days on his calendar: today and *that day.*

Most of us reading this book have been blessed with far more than the vast majority of people who ever lived. We find it hard to believe because we know plenty of people who have more or earn more than we do. The fact remains that when compared to the condition of people around the world, even lower-income Americans are considered wealthy. And, in the words of Erwin Lutzer, "We will be judged on the basis of our loyalty to Christ with the time, talents, and treasures *that were at our disposal*" (emphasis added).[2]

Most importantly, our Lord Jesus makes an observation about where we will stand in the judgment: "From everyone who has been given much, much will be demanded; and from the one who has been entrusted with much, much more will be asked" (Luke 12:48, NIV).

The coming judgment motivates us to seek God's will for every aspect of our lives, including our finances. Page after page in Scripture echoes this theme of accountability.

3. Time is short; eternity is long.
Understanding the brevity of time is a hallmark of the faithful manager. "Do not boast about tomorrow, for you do not know what a day may bring forth" (Proverbs 27:1). Planning is not wrong; on the contrary, faithfulness requires that we use God-given wisdom to prepare for the future. However, the faithful manager is not fooled into thinking she will work and save and strive for that magical day in the future when she can finally focus on God's purpose in her life. She sees the danger in putting off the responsibility to live for Christ now. The life abandoned to God's purpose, the life of no regrets, can only be lived with the view that each day could be our last on earth. Eternity stretches out before us.

4. The pursuit of material riches is not a valid goal in and of itself.
There is nothing wrong with having money. The Bible is full of godly men and women who were wealthy, including Abraham and Job. The question is one of purpose. We can spend money in many ways for our personal benefit. It can buy a certain lifestyle, new houses and cars, and vacations. Eventually, however, the question becomes, "Now what?" The richest man who ever lived, Solomon, said it best:

> I denied myself nothing my eyes desired; I refused my heart
> no pleasure. My heart took delight in all my work, and this
> was the reward for all my labor. Yet when I surveyed all that

my hands had done and what I had toiled to achieve, every-thing was meaningless, a chasing after the wind; nothing was gained under the sun. (Ecclesiastes 2:10-11, NIV)

God has gifted some people with the ability to generate money. They have become wealthy by His grace and providence. The question for them becomes, "What should I do now with His resources?" John Galsworthy puts it this way: "Wealth is a means to an end, not the end itself. As a synonym for health and happiness, it has had a fair trial and failed dismally."[3] One of life's greatest ironies is that many people spend their entire lives chasing after wealth only to find that most of the truly rewarding things in life have little to do with money. The wealthy learn this by experience. Those who are the happiest find purpose in their work, helping others, or some other meaningful activity.

Rich or poor, the faithful manager looks to God as the owner and master, and looks to money as a means to accomplish His eternal purposes.

5. God has two objectives for money.

Scripture is an invaluable reference tool for the faithful manager because he or she wants to know as much as possible about God's plan for money. While there is more in the Bible on money and material possessions than almost any other topic, it can be boiled down to two priorities: *invest in family and invest in others.* That's it. Care for your family and help others.

VISION

FINANCIAL VALUES

1. Invest in family
2. Invest in others

We have now reviewed some of the values shared by faithful managers: All wealth belongs to God, we are accountable for how we use it, time is short, pursuit of riches is not a valid goal, and God wants us to invest in family and others.

Remember, in our investing equation, *values* translate into *vision* based on a desire for *rewards.* So what rewards are in view as we evaluate God's two priorities for money?

> To lay up treasure in heaven, we must invest in what will be there—God and people. *David Wills*

REWARDS FOR INVESTING IN FAMILY

The Bible does not say much about rewards for investing financially in family, yet most of us spend almost all of our resources in this area. Why is that?

The first reason is obvious: We face the results on a daily basis. There is a natural sense of responsibility to provide for family that is enforced by the realities of life. In other words, God does not need to tell you to feed your children; they let you know they're hungry. However, we are reminded of this obligation in 1 Timothy 5:8: "But if anyone does not provide for his own, and especially for those of his household, he has denied the faith and is worse than an unbeliever." Paul was teaching the church how to care for the poor, and he wanted to emphasize the primary responsibility to support family members.

The second reason we readily use money for ourselves and our families is that we have a clear view of the reward. I think ahead to when my children will be independent and hopefully well adjusted, with families of their own. I think about them receiving good educations and maybe even some inheritance when I'm gone. I have a vision of financial independence for my wife, Melissa, and me one day. Although I enjoy working in my business, there may come a time when we would like to be able to pursue other things without requiring any outside income.

It is easy for me to focus my finances in this area because I can readily understand the rewards for investing in my family. *The obligation side of the equation keeps me going on the tough days, but it is a very real vision of the future reward that empowers me with passion to achieve the goal.*

How is this desire for rewards reflected in my vision for investing? It turns my values into a road map for how to get where I want to go. If you'll look at the expanded investing equation (next page), you'll see how this plays out.

For most people, the vision for investing in their family starts to become much clearer after about age forty. At that point, their passion (or panic, as the case may be) drives them to look for a wise financial strategy to achieve their goals. They are ready to focus on what I refer to in this book as the

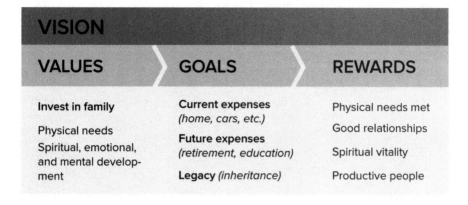

VISION		
VALUES	**GOALS**	**REWARDS**
Invest in family	**Current expenses** *(home, cars, etc.)*	Physical needs met
Physical needs		Good relationships
Spiritual, emotional, and mental develop-ment	**Future expenses** *(retirement, education)*	Spiritual vitality
	Legacy *(inheritance)*	Productive people

Family Portfolio. This is commonly known as financial planning or managing your money.

As the name suggests, the Family Portfolio is a long-term strategy to provide money for the physical and developmental needs of the family. A definition of *needs* is very important in this process, and it should be the topic of much prayer and thoughtful consideration (more on that in chapter 4).

A great deal has been written about personal finance for Christians, and it is a critical part of being a faithful manager. Because our everyday lives are so complex, most people do have a general idea that they need to plan in this area.

STRATEGY
(Discipline
+
Wisdom)

Creating and executing a wise strategy starts with discipline, and discipline starts with planning. Careful planning involves understanding three things: (1) your current situation, (2) where you want to go, and (3) how to get there. Furthermore, a disciplined manager understands his or her limits and seeks wise counsel as needed. When you formulate a strategy, all areas of the family finances need to line up with your goals.

We have talked about the vision part of the investing equation. Now let's look at how the strategy maps out:

STRATEGY		
DISCIPLINE	**Issues/Tools**	**WISDOM**
Planning	Budgeting	Bible/Prayer/Holy Spirit
Communicating	Income Taxes	Advisors
Spending	Loans	Experience
Saving	Business	Books and other resources
Paying off debt	Investments	
	Risk management	
	Estates & trusts	

Formulating an effective strategy is a detailed and time-consuming process. It is, however, necessary for those who seek the rewards. Keep in mind that your Family Portfolio strategy should be dynamic. Even though many pieces of the plan will remain the same over time, periodic review and adjustments are essential to the long-term health of the portfolio.

WHAT ABOUT INVESTING IN OTHERS?

Wait, we missed something. Isn't charitable giving part of my family's financial picture? Shouldn't it be included in the strategy outlined above? Well, yes and no.

At one time I thought of giving as little more than a "random act of kindness." We gave money to our church because Melissa and I learned as children to give at least 10 percent of our income back to God. If we felt particularly moved by the needs of a family or a missionary and there was room left in our budget, we would give a little more. Over the years we donated lots of clothes and old stuff to Goodwill and put a few dollars in the Salvation Army bucket at Christmas. There was never much thought involved and certainly no planning.

Maybe you can relate to this. If you have been a Christian for any length of time, you probably have developed some feelings about giving. Unfortunately, many people feel resentful that pastors and nonprofit organizations always seem to be asking for money. The giving that actually occurs is more often from a sense of guilt than from purpose or compassion, and it almost never involves any strategic planning. Why do you think that is true? If giving to others is one of God's two main purposes for money, why is this priority not lived out in the life of the average Christian? Could it be we don't understand that giving is an investment? Could it be we don't understand the rewards?

We'll investigate this further in the next chapter.

DISCUSSION QUESTIONS

1. How do you react to this statement: "God has a plan for your life, including your money, and you will be held accountable for faithfulness to His plan"?

2. In today's society, what does a faithful manager look like? How does he or she live within your culture?

3. What values drive your thinking and actions about possessions, family, work, investing, and giving? Is there a disconnect between what you know to be the "correct" answers and the way you are actually living?

4. Consider the idea that investing is only a means to an end and that all of our earthly goals are truly short-term in light of eternity. How does that impact your financial priorities?

5. How important is it to you to invest in your family?

6. What are your views on giving and investing in others? Have you spent any time studying what the Bible says about giving? How can you be more intentional in this area of your life?

2

The Ultimate Investment

- Investing in others: obligation or opportunity?
- Eternal rewards—now and to come
- Should a Christian seek eternal rewards?
- Giving as the ultimate investment

Twenty-seven years is all it took. After reading the Bible since 1975 and studying and working as a financial advisor for more than a decade, it came to me: Giving is the ultimate long-term investment. It just made sense. Investment returns well above what could ever be found elsewhere, no risk of default, returns compounded *forever*, benefits to be enjoyed even more *after* this life—Wow! It may have taken me a while to catch on, but now the idea had my attention.

We ended the previous chapter by asking why people are not motivated to invest in others by *giving*. If giving is the ultimate investment, why are so few people motivated by it?

INVESTING IN OTHERS: OBLIGATION OR OPPORTUNITY?

In chapter 1 we noted that God has two priorities for money: investing in family and investing in others. Most of us have a good handle on the first one. For me and for many others, the confusion came into play with the "investing in others" part. Why? Two reasons. First, I did not realize the priority God places on giving. Second, I had never understood the opportunity for rewards.

ALIGNING WITH GOD'S PRIORITIES

I had always seen giving as a *part of my Family Portfolio*. In other words, giving was in the same category as paying off the mortgage, paying the utilities, educating my children, and saving for the future. The picture looked something like this:

GOD'S PRIORITIES FOR MONEY?

After studying the issue in depth, however, I have come to realize that giving is actually a separate category, consistent with the top-level priority God places on money. This new paradigm of giving is more accurately represented as:

Therefore, I believe there are two parts to a person's financial situation—the Family Portfolio and the Eternity Portfolio. Although interrelated, each is distinctive in its focus.

GOD'S PRIORITIES FOR MONEY

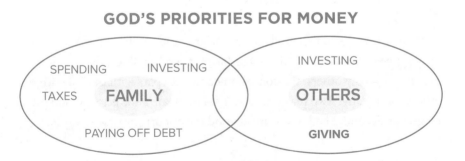

OBLIGATION OR OPPORTUNITY?

The second problem with my view on giving was that I didn't see the opportunity for rewards. Instead, I saw giving as taking away money that could be spent on me or my family. It was hard to get real excited about that.

Most of what I have read and heard about giving portrays it as the *obligation* of every Christian. That is accurate at one level, since much of what is said in the Bible about giving conveys a message of responsibility.

I feel the obligation to give based on at least three realities in my life. First, I give out of a sense of gratitude for what God has done for me and how He has provided for my needs. Second, I give to show my love for God in worship of Him. Third, I give as a tangible fulfillment of my responsibility to love other people, to help provide for their needs. Each of these is a biblical obligation. According to the Bible, these sacrifices are pleasing to God. Hebrews 13:16 reinforces this: "But do not forget to do good and to share, for with such sacrifices God is well pleased."

> I wish to add *joy* to the obligation and opportunity of giving. I have come to realize that one of the great joys of life is giving to others.
>
> *Dr. Johnny Hunt*

> It seems there are 3 main motivators in scripture: Fear (reverence), Love, and Rewards.
>
> *David Wills*

> Far from being an obligation, giving is a "disciplined passion." A generous giver told me once that when he gets a windfall bonus or profit, "We don't go shopping at the mall, we go shopping in the world."
>
> *Todd Harper*

However, there is something much bigger that makes me passionate about my giving as an *opportunity*. Much of what is written in Scripture about giving speaks about the upside, the reward for those who give to help others. There is very little in the Bible about rewards for investing for yourself and your family. Why is that? Is giving more important in God's eyes than meeting my family's needs? I don't think so. The answer lies within human nature.

Earlier we asked why giving is not a priority for most Christians. *The answer is that obligation alone is not enough to give us a **vision** for investing in others.*

What was it in our investing equation that transformed values to vision? *The desire for rewards.* God knew that with few exceptions the Family Portfolio would take care of itself because we can see the rewards. He also knew that we tend to be inwardly focused, and unless He specifically told us there would be rewards for being generous to others, the thought might not even cross our minds. So He inspired the writers of Scripture to say a great deal about the rewards for giving.

God wants us to take this second priority for money just as seriously as the first. He wants to change our hearts and give us a desire for the personal rewards of investing in others.

Why do we need a change of heart? Remember that vision for investing starts with our values, which show most clearly what is important to us. Dr. Bruce Wilkinson once said that the things you do are directly connected to where your heart is, as if by a rubber band. Although you can make temporary adjustments where your actions move away from your heart, after a time they always snap back. True life change must begin with a heart change.

According to Matthew 6:21, "Where your treasure is, there your heart will be also," where we place our treasure reflects our values (heart). A good way to figure out if you need a heart change is to take a look through your bank statement or expense log/check register. You'll quickly see where you're putting your treasure and can assess whether that is where you want your heart to be.

I talked with a young woman who was trying to get her finances in order about this treasure/heart principle, and together we looked through her last few bank statements. Other than expenses for her rent and regularly monthly bills, she was putting most of her treasure at Nordstrom, Starbucks, and the frozen yogurt place near her office. She was quite shocked at how many transactions were for those three places. I asked if that was where she wanted her heart to be, and we discussed practical ways for her to get her treasure instead to the places where her heart was.

Heather Tuininga

How does a change of heart in the area of giving come about? It starts with faith and believing God. As the Scripture verse says, "Faith comes by hearing, and hearing by the word of God" (Romans 10:17). Life change takes heart change, which takes faith, which takes hearing the Word! In this particular passage Paul was referring specifically to faith in Jesus Christ as Savior; however, faith is equally applicable as we try to develop a vision for the proper use of our possessions. The writer of Hebrews describes this "temporal versus eternal" perspective as Moses viewed it:

> By faith Moses, when he had grown up, refused to be known as the son of Pharaoh's daughter. He chose to be mistreated along with the people of God rather than to enjoy the pleasures of sin for a short time. He regarded disgrace for the sake of Christ as *of greater value than the treasures of Egypt, because he was looking ahead to his reward.* (Hebrews 11:24-26, NIV, emphasis added)

So the faith of Moses gave him the vision for the *reward*, which he viewed as more valuable than all the treasures of ancient Egypt! Our faith, and therefore our vision, comes by hearing what God has written about the incredible opportunity of giving.

THE GENEROSITY ECOSYSTEM

Often we think of generosity in two traditional ways—either as a simple act of charitable kindness, like giving a meal to a homeless person or making a tax-deductible donation at church. But giving doesn't occur in a vacuum, nor is it confined to these conventional ways of thinking. It might be helpful to discuss how this fits into what I describe as the *Generosity Ecosystem*. Jesus showed us the way when He lived on earth as the ultimate giver. He gave healing, hope, wisdom, and then, finally, His very life for our priceless benefit. He was continuing His Father's activity—giving to create and sustain life. It is a comprehensive view of generosity from a kingdom perspective.

First, the resources have to come from somewhere. A chain of value creation originates with our Creator, who supplies natural laws, natural resources, unique abilities (including creativity itself), relationships, and sometimes even divine intervention.

Second, God's system on earth requires people to do something. They must give of themselves in myriad ways to create results, even as basic as finding food each day. Often, this giving is with explicit expectation of reward—filling our bellies, earning an income, having a place to live, and so on. We cannot shy away from the basic law of giving for reward. And before you jump to call that "earning" instead of "giving," where we denigrate the former and attribute spiritual piety to the latter, pause for a moment. Consider that human beings, when we truly boil down our definitions, may not have the capacity for pure altruism. Maybe just a scale that runs from base self-interest to Spirit-filled self-interest? When I think of my best impulses to sacrifice for others or serve out of a pure love for God, the deeper I dig the more discomfort I feel about the purity of my motives. Remember, there are emotional motives and spiritual motives too. Even when, at my most legitimately selfless posture, I give "because I love God," isn't there still gain to me? I receive love, joy, peace! Let's honestly consider that God is the only selfless giver and let ourselves off the hook. He designed the system and actually encourages self-interest in specific directions (more on that to come). Importantly, we should be extremely careful about how we judge other's motives.

Third, as we "do something," there is opportunity for generosity in the doing. Time and unique abilities have incredible redemptive potential. It may be that the work itself is serving an intended beneficiary (e.g., certain volunteer activities), or we find numerous ways to exercise generosity to co-workers, employees, or vendors. There are, of course, obligations and duties—we owe certain things. But above and beyond the requirements, there are daily opportunities to show God's love through our generous spirits in the doing.

Fourth, in God's economic system, He uses our needs, desires, creativity, and compassion to give us purpose and motivation to build organizations (for profit and not- for-profit) that provide for our needs and those of others.

And fifth, there are often "net" financial resources that come as a result of our efforts. This money, which must be spent on our families, reinvested for our future use, or given and invested for the benefit of others, represents the focal point of the book.

Thinking through the generosity ecosystem leads to expanded and exciting ways we can be about God's business with both our personal resources (time, unique abilities, relationships) and our financial resources (money). We begin to see the vital linkage of God's specific calling to our greatest impact. This understanding leads us to clear thinking about new models of giving, like social entrepreneurship and venture philanthropy. The methods and packaging will continue to change through time, but the ecosystem remains.

When I think about investing in others, it really covers a broad yet practical spectrum across my personal life (close friends, acquaintances) spheres of influence (business, kids' school, ministries) and beyond (global poor, justice). [Because of their broad reach] business and social entrepreneurship are important ways of investing in others. Besides job creation, many products can be developed that relieve suffering and advance the welfare of others while creating value. For example, four years ago I invested in a startup for a medical device that allows people with AIDS and other mutating diseases in poor countries and rural areas to be tested more frequently and at a small fraction of the price. This, in turn, helps them to get treated more effectively.

Jack Alexander

ETERNAL REWARDS—NOW AND TO COME

We defined the *values* of the faithful manager in the first chapter, but what about the *rewards?* The Bible is full of God's promises to His faithful children. Rewards both now and forever are in store for those who love and obey Him. Perhaps more surprisingly, the Bible teaches that Christians can *increase or decrease* eternal rewards based on their faithfulness in life.

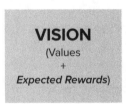

VISION
(Values
+
Expected Rewards)

In his book *Your Eternal Rewards*, Erwin Lutzer writes, "The person you are today will determine the rewards you will receive tomorrow. Those who are pleasing to Christ will be generously rewarded; those who are not pleasing to Him will receive negative consequences and a lesser reward. In other words, your life *here* will impact your life *there* forever."[1]

> Thinking influences actions. The most generous people I know have fully adopted this perspective of an Eternity Portfolio. They intentionally use their giving as an amazing opportunity to invest in God's kingdom.
>
> *Todd Harper*

Nowhere in Scripture is the connection between our actions in this life and eternal rewards more clearly described than in the area of giving. Over and over, the Bible makes the case that those who are generous with this world's resources will be blessed by God both in this life and in all eternity. Let's look at a sample of what the Bible says about rewards for giving.

In the words of Solomon, the wisest man who ever lived:

> Honor the Lord with your possessions, and with the firstfruits of all your increase; so your barns will be filled with plenty, and your vats will overflow with new wine. (Proverbs 3:9–10)

> The world of the generous gets larger and larger; the world of the stingy gets smaller and smaller. The one who blesses others is abundantly blessed; those who help others are helped. (Proverbs 11:24–25, MSG)

> He who has a generous eye will be blessed, for he gives of his bread to the poor. (Proverbs 22:9)

In the words of Paul, who wrote much of the New Testament:

> Remember this: Whoever sows sparingly will also reap sparingly, and whoever sows generously will also reap generously. Each man should give what he has decided in his heart to give, not reluctantly or under compulsion, for God loves a cheerful giver. And God is able to make all grace abound to you, so that in all things at all times, having all that you need, you

will abound in every good work. As it is written: "He has scattered abroad his gifts to the poor; his righteousness endures forever."

Now he who supplies seed to the sower and bread for food will also supply and increase your store of seed and will enlarge the harvest of your righteousness. You will be made rich in every way so that you can be generous on every occasion, and through us your generosity will result in thanksgiving to God. (2 Corinthians 9:6-11, NIV)

And, in the words of Jesus Christ Himself:

Everyone who has given up houses or brothers or sisters or father or mother or children or property, for my sake, will receive a hundred times as much in return and will have eternal life. (Matthew 19:29, NLT)

Give, and it will be given to you: good measure, pressed down, shaken together, and running over will be put into your bosom. For with the same measure that you use, it will be measured back to you. (Luke 6:38)

These represent just a handful of the many biblical references. But do you get the sense that God wants to encourage giving? If we look specifically for the rewards promised in Scripture, we will be amazed at just how many there are.

Philippians 2:7 says Jesus humbled himself and became like a servant to reach us. As an entrepreneur, I naturally think about looking for opportunities and getting an advantage for my capital. But with my giving and serving, I flip that, looking to disadvantage myself to invest in His kingdom.

Jack Alexander

WHAT ARE ETERNAL REWARDS?

First and foremost, let me say that nothing in this book should be construed to advocate the so-called "prosperity theology" of giving. God has not promised to give you a Lexus, a beach house, or an easy retirement if you are faithful in giving. He has not even promised to reward you *in this lifetime.* Although it is abundantly clear that we will be rewarded based on our faithfulness, what is not as clear is the *nature* and *timing* of those rewards.

God *has* promised faithful givers a variety of non-financial/material rewards that WILL come in this lifetime, including more resources to give, increased righteousness, experiencing other people thanking God for His provision, and knowing the joy of meeting others' needs and investing in God's work. (See 2 Corinthians 9:10-12 and Malachi 3:10.)

If you've ever been led by God to invest in something eternal, you've tasted the joy He wants us to experience by engaging in His work. As we create and refine our Eternity Portfolios, I pray it results in even more joy and thanksgiving to God.

Heather Tuininga

From a timing standpoint, we need to realize that our lives on earth are only a fraction of our eternal existence. Think of examples such as the beggar Lazarus in the Bible (Luke 16:19–31) and the martyred saints described in Hebrews 11 who never received their reward in life.

However, there are also many examples in Scripture of God's current blessings. Much of the reward for giving that was promised in the Old Testament related to increased crops and herds as well as protection from enemies—all of which related to physical rewards during life on earth.

My personal experience has convinced me that God can certainly choose to bless faithful giving during this life. Many others would agree. Listen to the testimony of a minister who lived in England in the 1600s:

> I dare challenge all the world to give me one instance, or at least any considerable number of instances of any truly merciful men, whose charity has undone them. But as living wells the more they are drawn, the more freely they spring and flow: so the substance of liberal men doth oftentimes, if not, ordinarily, multiply in the very distribution: even as the five loaves and few fishes did multiply in their distribution by the hands of the Redeemer. And the widow's oil increased by pouring it out for the holy prophet.[2]

Reverend Thomas Gouge personally lived out this testimony as he funded his own ministry as well as helping many poor people in his area using the estate left by his father.

So God can choose to bless our giving in this world with increased material possessions. But what if He does not? Most of the verses about eternal rewards do not mention money or material possessions as rewards for giving. Instead, they mention rewards in heaven. These seem to fall into three main categories:

- **Crowns**: "Now there is in store for me the crown of righteousness, which the Lord, the righteous Judge, will award to me on that day—and not only to me, but also to all who have longed for his appearing" (2 Timothy 4:8, NIV). See also James 1:12, 1 Peter 5:4, and Revelation 2:10.
- **Treasure**: "Provide purses for yourselves that will not wear out, a treasure in heaven that will not be exhausted, where no thief comes near and no moth destroys" (Luke 12:33, NIV). See also Matthew 6:20, Mark 10:21, 1 Timothy 6:19.
- **Positions of authority**: "If we endure, we will also reign with him" (2 Timothy 2:12, NIV). Also see Matthew 19:28 and Revelation 3:21.

Without question, the rewards for Christians who are faithful in this life will be great. *This includes faithfulness with their material possessions.*

Several great books on eternity and eternal rewards are available. Christian writers throughout history have commented about eternal rewards (see Appendix E). Though we will not know for certain in advance what each of these rewards will be like, the emphasis placed on obtaining them should make us excited about the prospect.

IS IT SELFISH FOR A CHRISTIAN TO SEEK ETERNAL REWARDS?
Should a Christian pursue God's favor and the prospect of being rewarded? Does that seem self-serving and maybe even covetous?

It is certainly possible to have wrong motives related to giving—or anything else we do as Christians, for that matter. This gives rise to what Paul refers to as "wood, hay, and straw" that will be burned at the judgment (1 Corinthians 3:8–15). However, Paul also talked a great deal about striving to obtain a crown, and he encouraged the early church to do the same.

This is not about obtaining heaven and eternal life. Paul was clear in his writings that salvation is by faith alone. Crowns and other rewards result from our actions here on earth. The fact is that our best interests are aligned with God's purpose and plan for our lives. Randy Alcorn puts it this way in his book *In Light of Eternity:*

> Though God's glory is the highest and ultimate reason for any course of action, Scripture sees no contradiction between God's eternal glory and our eternal good. On the contrary, glorifying God will always result in our greatest eternal good. Likewise, pursuing our eternal good—as he commands us to—will always glorify God.[3]

THE DEBATE CONTINUES:
IS IT SELFISH TO WANT REWARDS?

Should I serve or give in expectation of a reward? Even if we're talking about eternal rewards, doesn't that seem like an un-Christian motive? This has been a burning question for followers of Christ since the very beginning. Didn't the apostle Peter himself say something to the effect of "We've left everything to follow You, now what do we get?" (see Matthew 19:27). The question was an honest and obvious one based on much of what Jesus said. *He continuously*

Continued on next page

promised benefits, a changed life, and eternal life for those who followed.

Much could be said on this topic, but I think the pendulum has swung too far, primarily as a reaction to legalism of the evangelical church in the 1960s–1980s. Namely, the idea of "doing anything" is treated suspiciously these days as being opposed to "grace." Then, the idea of "doing something to get something" is even further out of favor. But is this taking a proper, Christian view of the realities of the world God created? Isn't it His privilege to design us to respond to rewards and give us a part in that process? Economically, I see this in the broad benefits to society of people creating value for others while serving their own interests. The providential, common grace of God operates to bring good in the world. At the most basic level, consider your body's response to hunger. God created your body to be fueled by food. In His created system, hunger motivates you to eat, and you have to work to get the food. Is it wrong to work for the reward of food? As I've said before, humans may not have the capacity for dispassionate pure altruism. We were created to respond to Him. Based on the many promises in Scripture, it seems we need prompting in the direction of generosity, and He wants us to respond to biblical motivation.

One final thought: *the greatest reward is knowing Him.* Our Father is kind to give us incentives and smaller rewards along the way, but Jesus taught us that eternal life—joy, peace, fulfillment—comes from knowing Him (John 17:3). Over the years I've found a progression in following Christ whereby taking very practical steps, based on motivation and instruction in Scripture, lead to a growing understanding of my heavenly Father. The more I know Him, the more I want to know and pursue those things that draw me closer. Getting to play a small role in His kingdom work, getting to see Him shape the world around me, watching lives change in response, realizing that all I truly desire is *in Him*—these are the ultimate rewards.

THE ULTIMATE INVESTMENT

If giving provides rewards for all eternity, and seeking eternal rewards does not conflict with God's will for us, shouldn't we be looking to give as much as possible? Doesn't this sound like a significant investment opportunity? Compared to other investments we can make during our lifetimes, which might produce rewards for thirty to forty years, the concept of eternal rewards is compelling.

Does Scripture provide a mandate for maximizing this ultimate investment opportunity? Apparently the apostle Paul thought so. As he raised money for the work of Christ in the first-century churches, he was thinking about investment return to the giver. Notice his words to the Philippian church:

> And you yourselves also know, Philippians, that at the first preaching of the gospel, after I departed from Macedonia, no church shared with me in the matter of giving and receiving but you alone; for even in Thessalonica you sent a gift more than once for my needs. Not that I seek the gift itself, *but I seek for the profit which increases to your account.* (Philippians 4:15–17, NASB, emphasis added)

Paul had just told the Philippians he had learned to be content in any situation, and he goes on to say he has everything he needs. His concern was for the givers. As they gave to further the kingdom of God, something happened: *profit increased to their account.* What account is that?

> A friend of mine asked me to join him in giving to a particular Christian charity. I told him my giving for the year was complete—that my wife and I plan our giving at the beginning of each year and we were done for that year. He said, "Well, I figure the faster I can convert this world's currency into heaven's currency, the better." I had to admit he had a point, and so we gave.
>
> *Lorne Jackson*

Before we draw conclusions, let's look at instructions Paul sends to Timothy for the church at Ephesus:

> Command those who are rich in this present age not to be haughty, nor to trust in uncertain riches but in the living God, who gives us richly all things to enjoy. Let them do good, that they be rich in good works, ready to give, willing to share, storing up for themselves a good foundation for the time to come, that they may lay hold on eternal life. (1 Timothy 6:17–19)

First, we should understand that to be "rich" in those days meant you had the bare essentials—food, clothing, shelter. So most of us would be included. Also note that there is nothing inherently wrong with being rich because God "gives us richly all things to enjoy." However, these people were advised to be abundant in good works for the purpose of storing up a foundation for themselves! MacArthur's Commentary interprets the original language this way:

> By sharing their earthly treasures with others, they are **storing up for themselves the treasure of a good foundation for the future.** Apothesaurizo (**storing up**) could be translated "amassing a treasure," while themelios (**foundation**) can refer to a fund. The rich are not to be concerned with getting a return on their investment in this life. Those who lay up treasure in heaven will be content to wait to receive their dividends in the future when they reach heaven.[4]

So Paul gives specific instructions to the Christians at Ephesus to give in order to accumulate eternal rewards. Where do you think Paul got the idea? He got it from Jesus Christ Himself. Many years before Paul even became a Christian, Jesus was preaching to the multitudes and said these words:

> Do not lay up for yourselves treasures on earth, where moth and rust destroy and where thieves break in and steal; but lay up for yourselves treasures in heaven, where neither moth nor rust destroys and where thieves do not break in and steal. For where your treasure is, there your heart will be also. (Matthew 6:19-21)

Possessions compete for our affections, taking our hearts away from God. Did Jesus command us not to lay up treasures? No. As Bruce Wilkinson has noted, Jesus was simply making the case that it is unwise to accumulate them where they will be destroyed. Even if we save them from robbers, rust, and insects, we will leave everything here when we die. Jesus was telling us to "lay up for [ourselves]" a stake in the ultimate financial investment.

The Bible says, "Do not lay up for *yourselves*" treasures. Does that mean it's all right to lay up treasure on earth for others? Maybe. I have always struggled with giving to endowments or long-term funds where that capital is held and invested to be given out later or used to earn income to be given out later. But maybe Jesus is saying it's okay to "lay up" treasures for others, just not for ourselves. But we should "lay up" for ourselves in heaven (converting this world's currency to heaven's currency).

Lorne Jackson

Jesus states the options: suffer loss by holding on to our possessions, or gain an incorruptible inheritance by giving them away. These verses, combined with many others, lead to an astonishing but unavoidable conclusion: We have the ability to influence our eternity in heaven based on the faithful use of money on earth, specifically in the area of giving.

Jonathan Edwards, one of the most famous American preachers of the eighteenth century, said it like this:

> What man, acting wisely and considerately, would concern himself much about laying up in store in such a world as this, and would not rather neglect this world, and let it go to them that would take it, and apply all his heart and strength to lay up treasure in heaven, and to press on to that world of love?[5]

How does this fit into our investing equation? We are beginning to form a vision for the rewards of investing in eternity. When I'm investing financially for my family, my primary motivation is *tangible rewards*, such as education or providing for physical needs. When it comes to investing financially in others, my primary motivation is *eternal rewards*. It is interesting to note that the rewards that motivate me to invest in family seem to be the *means* of achieving the rewards in giving to others (see chart). We should see no conflict between what God wants of us in life (loving others) and the rewards for being faithful to the task.

It is not always greed but sometimes lack of vision that leads most of us to accumulate and spend money in this world instead of laying up treasure

VISION

VALUES	GOALS	REWARDS
Invest in family	Current expenses *(home, cars, etc.)*	Physical needs met
Physical needs	Future expenses *(retirement, education)*	Good relationships
Spiritual, emotional, and mental development	Legacy *(inheritance)*	Spiritual vitality
		Productive people
Invest in others	Physical needs met	ETERNAL REWARDS
Physical needs	Good relationships	• Treasures in Heaven
Spiritual, emotional, and mental development	Spiritual vitality	• Crowns
	Productive people	• Positions of authority

in heaven. God has appealed to our own enlightened self-interest by promising eternal rewards in the area of giving, in effect making it the ultimate investment. This approach benefits God's kingdom purposes and accrues to our ultimate good.

> Is it possible that lack of vision results in greed?
>
> *David Wills*

Once we catch the vision, the questions start: Does the Bible really offer guidance on strategic giving? How much should I give, or better yet, how much should I keep? How much is enough for my family? How do I choose where to give? Will my gifts be used effectively for the kingdom? How can I involve my family in this strategy and teach my children to give generously?

What we need is a strategy, a plan that will empower us to be faithful managers.

We need the Eternity Portfolio.

DISCUSSION QUESTIONS

1. How do you think of giving—as obligation or opportunity? What is that based on? How would God have you look at it?

2. Do you believe God rewards Christians who are faithful with the time, abilities, and possessions He entrusts to their care? Can we earn rewards?

3. Can a Christian lose rewards because of unfaithfulness in this life?

4. Have you ever thought about the nature of eternity, heaven, and eternal rewards? What passages in the Bible have shaped your thinking in this area?

5. Why do you believe it is difficult for Christians today to focus on eternity and laying up treasures in heaven as opposed to in this world?

6. Are you open to the possibility that God may have a plan for you to give more than you ever thought you could or would? How would He communicate that to you? How would you accomplish it?

7. How much should you keep?

3

The Eternity Portfolio

■ The virtues of being intentional
■ Biblical guidance for successful giving
■ Overview of the Eternity Portfolio strategy

Years ago I began to notice an unusual similarity between my work with traditional investment portfolios and the strategy I had prepared for another area of my personal finances—giving. Eventually I realized that the principles were almost completely interchangeable.

As a result, my family has begun to view our giving as investing. The churches, ministries, and individuals we support make up our Eternity Portfolio of kingdom investments. The Bible is our guide for maximizing that portfolio.

The unique paradox of the Eternity Portfolio is that instead of saving and accumulating money, we are actively trying to give it away to God's glory, to follow Christ's teaching to "lay up treasures in heaven." As Pastor John MacArthur explains:

> It is possible that both our treasures on earth and our treasures in heaven can involve money and other material things. Possessions that are wisely, lovingly, willingly, and generously used for Kingdom purposes can be a means of accumulating heavenly possessions. When they are hoarded and stored, however, they not only become a spiritual hindrance but are subject to loss through moth, rust, and thieves.[1]

Although giving is certainly not the only way of laying up treasures in heaven, it seems to be one of the best ways of *investing money* for the really long term. The Eternity Portfolio is a personal strategy for being intentional about investing financial resources in those things that generate eternal treasure in heaven.

THE VIRTUES OF BEING INTENTIONAL

Early in our marriage, Melissa and I spent little time thinking about our giving strategy. We made donations in reaction to opportunities (or obligations!), without much planning or accountability. We subconsciously justified this spontaneity by overplaying the rationale that giving should be done "as the Spirit leads."

As we began to view our giving more seriously, however, I started thinking, *No one would argue that good planning for family finances is unspiritual.* In fact, I tell folks all the time that it is just prudent stewardship. In our churches we plan everything from small group strategy to airplane reservations for mission trips. Is that unspiritual? Of course not. Reverend Samuel Harris wrote more than 150 years ago about systematic giving:

> System always promotes efficiency. What would become of a man's worldly business, if he managed it without system, never executing a plan or making an investment till solicited, and abandoning labor to the control of impulse or convenience? And can he hope for any better results from a like disregard of system as a steward of God? From such lack of order, what but embarrassment and failure can result to the enterprises of benevolence? And what shall we say of those professors of Christ's religion who show so thorough an understanding of the necessity of system in worldly business, so utter a neglect of it in their contributions to benevolence: who are full of forethought and anxious calculation to realize the utmost of worldly acquisition; deliberate and far-sighted in planning, cautious in executing, lynx-eyed to discern an opportunity of gain, exact to the last fraction in their accounts, but heedless and planless in all they do for charity? Verily, "the children of this world are wiser in their generation than the children of light"; but "the children of light"

show no lack of that wisdom, till they come to use property for the benefit of others than themselves.[2]

> Intentional giving gripped me thirteen years ago when I first read this book. I began to be intentional with all I was entrusted with beyond my set budget. I began to realize that the extras in my life were not always given so I could *"live better"* but often so I could *"give greater."*
>
> *Dr. Johnny Hunt*

> Generosity is a spiritual discipline, and like other spiritual disciplines, it is not easy.
>
> *Larry Powell*

Jesus encouraged His disciples to be shrewd in using wealth as a means to achieve heavenly goals (see Luke 16:1–12). The book of Proverbs speaks of the benefits of planning, wise counsel, and diligence in managing life. It seems clear that the Christian life is a balance of prudent planning and faith. In my experience, there are at least four major benefits to having a strategic plan for your giving.

1. Planning maximizes giving—and leads to more effective giving.

Lack of clarity is the enemy of investing. For example, there is nothing like viewing your retirement plan in the cold light of day to get you motivated to invest. Seeing the numbers on paper highlights the difference between where you are financially and where you want to be. The same is true in giving. Once you start to formulate goals and measure results, your momentum builds, allowing you to discover ways to give more than you ever thought possible.

Planning also brings accountability. As the investor, you not only have expectations of yourself but you also look more closely at the effectiveness of the organizations you support.

> The process of planning creates clarity, and clarity results in purpose. Purpose reduces fear and brings more clarity.
>
> *David Wills*

2. Planning makes it easier to say no.

This may sound strange in light of the theme of this book, but being able to say no is one of the most freeing concepts you can learn. Without a giving plan, you can easily feel guilty whenever you have an opportunity to make a donation. "Should I be doing more?" "I haven't given anything to them in a while." "It *is* a really good cause." Sometimes you don't think you should give but you don't feel right saying no either.

I want to be open to spontaneous giving opportunities as the Lord leads me. However, when we have prayerfully and thoughtfully planned where the majority of our giving should be invested, we can honestly and freely tell someone that we are fully committed in that area and cannot help at this time.

> Have the freedom to say no: "What you're doing is a wonderful work for God's kingdom, but it's not what he's put on my heart."
>
> *Larry Powell*

3. Planning makes you a cheerful giver.

Each day you are confronted with the lure of instant gratification. There is seemingly no end to the ways you can use your money to fulfill a desire you have *right now*. Investing is not easy; it takes discipline to set aside money for the long term. A giving plan forces you to make that decision ahead of time so you don't have to make it a thousand times each month. This is why 401(k) plans and other automated savings plans are so effective. The participants understand that those funds are not available for spending and learn to manage their budgets accordingly.

Those who plan their giving have a different decision to make when an opportunity is presented. It's not as much about giving or keeping. They are energized and joyful when looking for investments because the money is already designated; it is no longer available for living expenses. The question then becomes: "Should I invest in this *particular* opportunity, and if so, how much?" Each day the habits of earning, spending, and saving money are reinforced in your life. Strategic planning makes your giving a habit as well.

You should determine beforehand how much you will give, then investigate opportunities God brings to invest those resources. Paul taught this to the early church (see 2 Corinthians 9:6-7). The Christians in Jerusalem were suffering because of famine and poverty, and Paul asked the Gentile churches to contribute to a fund he would deliver to the church in Jerusalem. He realized that if the Corinthians did not plan their gifts ahead, they would make other commitments with the resources and be resentful when he came to receive their gift. Cheerful giving results from planning.

4. Planning helps you understand where faith begins.

Although some would tell you it takes faith to give away *anything*, most of us have a certain level of discretionary income we can give away without much sacrifice or faith. As a result of prudent planning, we gain a new sensitivity to the amount of giving that will test our faith and keep us properly dependent on God.

I hope you see some of the benefits that result from planning your giving. Building your Eternity Portfolio is not a rigid process but an individual plan based on prayer, Scripture, and God's leading. It will be different for each family and will most certainly change over time. As a start, God has given us principles in Scripture that apply to giving, and He has provided intellect, sound reasoning, and faith to work out the details. We should start our plan by looking at the basics of successful giving as taught in the Bible.

We're called to give both cheerfully (2 Corinthians 9:7) and sacrificially (2 Corinthians 8:3, Proverbs 21:26). Think of this like a spectrum or slider bar with cheerful at one end and sacrificial at the other. Your sliding marker falls somewhere in between representing your current giving. You can assess whether your marker needs to be moved toward one

Continued on next page

end or the other as you assess whether your current giving is the right mix of sacrificial and cheerful.

One person I counseled was delighted to be giving to her church every week, however, she mentioned that her giving was somewhere between $10-50, depending on what was in her wallet. When we looked at her income and the other places she was putting her treasure, this was clearly not a sacrificial amount. So she was likely a bit too cheerful and not sacrificial enough and needed to move her marker closer to the sacrificial end.

On the other hand, if a single mom is giving so much that she's worried about feeding her children next week (and therefore not very cheerful), she should move her marker toward the cheerful end and find a place that allows her to feel both cheerful and sacrificial about her giving.

To discern whether your marker is at the right mix of both cheerful and sacrificial, ask:
- Do I love my current giving plan, the amounts I'm giving, and the places I'm giving? (Yes = cheerful)
- Am I worried about paying my housing or grocery costs if I give this money? (Yes = not cheerful)
- Am I missing out on something else I could have or experience by giving this money? (Yes = sacrificial)
- Am I giving God what's left in my wallet instead of giving Him my first and best, setting aside a set amount from my income? (Yes = likely not sacrificial)

Heather Tuininga

WE ALL PLAN FOR THINGS THAT MATTER; LET'S MAKE GIVING ONE OF THEM.

Some people are naturally more inclined to planning than others, but we all do at least some planning for the things that really matter in our lives. The degree and intensity of planning will vary, but, for example, I don't know anyone who regularly just shows up at the airport and then picks a flight to go on vacation. Here's a thought: *Use at least as much planning in your giving strategy as you do in other important areas of your life—like planning your kids' education, family vacations, or your retirement.*

BIBLICAL GUIDANCE FOR SUCCESSFUL GIVING

When it comes to managing your finances, three principles embody the accumulated wisdom of the ages: *spend less than you earn, avoid debt,* and *save for the future.* These are not rules you *must* obey. Calamity will not necessarily befall you for breaking them. However, over time, these principles lead to *greater reward.* In other words, you may finish the race without them, but you probably won't place in the top ten.

Likewise, when it comes to investing for eternity, God has given us principles that help achieve the greater reward. The writings of the apostle Paul give us most of the guidance in this area, and he emphasizes two main themes: motives and methods.

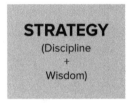

STRATEGY
(Discipline
+
Wisdom)

MOTIVES

The overwhelming theme of the Bible is God's love for us and how we should respond to that love—both to Him and to others. The way we handle our money is no exception. Paul speaks to the heart of the matter as he gives instruction to the church at Corinth:

> And now, brothers, we want you to know about the grace that God has given the Macedonian churches. Out of the most severe trial, *their overflowing joy and their extreme poverty welled up in rich generosity.* For I testify that they gave as much as they were able, and even beyond their ability. Entirely on their own, they urgently pleaded with us for the privilege of

sharing in this service to the saints. And they did not do as we expected, but *they gave themselves first to the Lord and then to us in keeping with God's will.* So we urged Titus, since he had earlier made a beginning, to bring also to completion this act of grace on your part. But just as you excel in everything—in faith, in speech, in knowledge, in complete earnestness and in your love for us— see that you also excel in this grace of giving.

I am not commanding you, but I want to test the sincerity of your love by comparing it with the earnestness of others. *For you know the grace of our Lord Jesus Christ, that though he was rich, yet for your sakes he became poor, so that you through his poverty might become rich.*

And here is my advice about what is best for you in this matter: Last year you were the first not only to give but also to have the desire to do so. Now finish the work, so that your eager willingness to do it may be matched by your completion of it, according to your means. *For if the willingness is there, the gift is acceptable according to what one has, not according to what he does not have.* (2 Corinthians 8:1–12, NIV, emphasis added)

So I thought it necessary to urge the brothers to visit you in advance and finish the arrangements for the generous gift you had promised. Then it will be ready as a generous gift, not as one grudgingly given.

Remember this: Whoever sows sparingly will also reap sparingly, and whoever sows generously will also reap generously. *Each man should give what he has decided in his heart to give, not reluctantly or under compulsion, for God loves a cheerful giver.* (2 Corinthians 9:5–7, NIV, emphasis added)

Paul speaks of a heart given first to the Lord and then to others. As Jesus Christ changes your heart, He changes your desires. One of those desires is to help others through giving freely. Notice how, by the grace of God, the poor Macedonians pleaded to make an investment in the kingdom that was beyond what they could afford.

This is not to say that, in the life of the Christian, God cannot use giving out of obligation. Giving that starts as a discipline, out of simple obedience, may over time be converted to cheerful willingness, and that is when the reward is maximized.

> This has certainly been true in my life. I grew up in a Christian home where I was taught to tithe on the first dollar I ever earned. I did this in the first part of my life more out of obligation than generosity. However, as I grew in understanding my role as a steward of God's resources, it became easier and easier to give more.
>
> *Lorne Jackson*

Motive is more important to God than amount. Even if we lack the ability to give a large amount, God judges motives when it comes to reward. "For if there is first *a willing mind*, it is accepted according to what one has, and not according to what he does not have" (2 Corinthians 8:12, emphasis added). Our overriding motives for giving should be a loving response to Christ's love for us and a tangible expression of our love for others.

In the Sermon on the Mount, Jesus taught what should *not* be the motive for our giving:

> Take heed that you do not do your charitable deeds before men, to be seen by them. Otherwise you have no reward from your Father in heaven. Therefore, when you do a charitable deed, do not sound a trumpet before you as the hypocrites do in the synagogues and in the streets, that they may have glory from men. Assuredly, I say to you, they have their reward. But when you do a charitable deed, do not let your left hand know what your right hand is doing, that your charitable deed may be in secret; and your Father who sees in secret will Himself reward you openly. (Matthew 6:1–4)

Note that Jesus is prompting us to the greater reward—the reward from the Father. Those who "give" with selfish motives have not really "given" at all. They have merely made a *purchase*, exchanging a charitable deed for the praise of men. If pride is the motivation behind our giving, we are making a purchase, not investing for the greater reward.

> Proper motives may even lead us to testify about our giving at times. Some people abuse the Scripture that teaches, "Do not let your left hand know what your right hand is doing" (Matthew 6:4), saying this means we should never talk about our giving. But, Jesus also criticized praying in public, yet we generally accept that as okay. Jesus was speaking to *motives* behind our prayers and our giving in public. In certain situations our giving needs to be public to let our light shine before men so they can glorify our Father. With right motives, we can humbly testify to God's faithfulness—not only to bring Him glory but also to encourage one another on to love and good deeds (Hebrews 10:24).
>
> *Todd Harper*

METHODS

When it comes to methods for giving, there are as many variations as there are Christians. However, according to Scripture, giving is to be *systematic, proportionate,* and *generous.* No passage sums it up better than this brief statement to the Corinthians.

> Now concerning the collection for the saints, as I have given orders to the churches of Galatia, so you must do also: On the first day of the week let each one of you lay something aside, storing up as he may prosper, that there be no collections when I come. (1 Corinthians 16:1-2)

I would add *first fruits* to *systematic, proportionate,* and *generous.* If we don't give to God first, we won't likely give Him much when we look at what's left over. I once had a pastor ask: If Jesus showed up for dinner, would you serve Him the freshest and best of whatever you had, or would you give him what's leftover? I don't think the way we give him our money should be any different.

Heather Tuininga

We have already discussed the merits of planning and being intentional about your giving strategy. Paul's instructions were to set something aside systematically, on a *regular basis.* He knew that if the Corinthians did not plan ahead, they would contribute small amounts grudgingly and out of obligation when he arrived.

"Storing up as he may prosper," or, in the New International Version, "in keeping with his income," seems to indicate that successful giving should be *in proportion* as God has blessed. This is further indicated in Jesus' observation of the widow's offering recorded in Mark 12:41–44. Jesus emphasized to His disciples that even though the widow gave only two pennies, she gave proportionately more than the others because it represented her whole livelihood.

One other principle to keep in mind about the methods for giving is the element of spontaneity. We should have a regular and proportionate plan for our ongoing investment, but at times we will be led to make extraordinary investments in opportunities that God reveals. These can be some of the most satisfying and exciting investments of all.

So there we have it—the general principles for building an Eternity Portfolio. If I were asked the secret to investing money for eternal rewards, I could sum it up no better than the following quote:

The Law of Charity
"And this law of charity lays itself on men in all varieties of condition, with an admirable equality of pressure. It requires each

to give according to his means, and according to his own judgment, formed with an enlightened conscience and a benevolent heart."[3]

Giving should be motivated by love; be done regularly, cheerfully, and discreetly; and be done in proportion to your wealth.

WHAT MAKES MONEY SO SPECIAL?

The concept of money is worth exploring a little further. I frequently hear Christians make statements about Time, Talent, and Treasure. Along the lines of "Generosity isn't just about money; I want to be generous with my time, talent, *and* treasure." However, money is different from treasure. *For most of us, money is all the Ts combined.* Unless you inherit the money, you typically acquire it through the use of your time and talent. So when you give of your money, you are truly giving of your time and talent! You have to work and serve others to get the money. And, critically, money has near-universal value to the recipient—it can be easily exchanged for whatever the recipient needs the most. Whereas my time and talents may or may not be valuable to a particular recipient (if they need a professional dancer for example, my time and talents would be less than worthless!), I know that a gift of money can be used to acquire exactly what is needed. Furthering the example, just because my time might be worth $500 per hour as an advisor, it most certainly isn't worth $500 per hour to an organization that needs a plumber. They would be far better off if I gave them $200 cash than if I spent the entire afternoon working on the plumbing.

God calls each of us to fulfill our different roles based on the varying gifts He has given us. For some, that could be meeting needs with direct effort—such as serving at the soup kitchen, planting trees, caring for orphans. Others are more often on the funding, strategy, or networking side of the operation. Each has an important part to play, and of course we all end up doing some direct service and some financial investment. But pride says, "My way is most important, and everyone should do it this way." Humility asks, "How can I be most useful to His kingdom given my abilities, resources, and the specifics of this situation?" Often it's *not* another set of hands that is needed. In fact, I've talked to a number of nonprofit leaders in recent days who worry they spend too much time making up jobs for volunteers, preventing them from accomplishing the purpose of the ministry. What they need is funding. And I think again: *the wealthiest Christians who've ever lived, even in the middle class* . . . A big part of our role in the kingdom is on the funding side.

Money is a different category. It's not my "treasure," like an antique golden cross or fancy car. For most people, money represents the rolled-up value they've created through time, hard work, creativity, and applying the talents God has given them. Don't be afraid to create more of it—*you are giving of yourself* when you provide necessary funding out of the money you've earned. If earning that money—while following the Spirit's leading in your priorities—keeps you from volunteering as much of your time, don't be "guilted" into giving up the stage God has called you to in the mistaken belief that only "hands-on ministry" matters. We don't need everyone playing on the same stage; we need all Christians serving *primarily* in their God-given roles.

Reminds me of a quote by former British Prime Minister Margaret Thatcher: "How could we respond to the many calls for help, or invest for the future, or support the wonderful artists or craftsmen whose work also glorifies God, unless we had first worked hard and used our talents to create the necessary wealth?"[4]

OVERVIEW OF THE ETERNITY PORTFOLIO STRATEGY

Now that we've reviewed some of the biblical principles behind money and giving, we'll move from the theoretical to the practical. The following chapters will guide you through the process of funding, designing, investing, and monitoring your own Eternity Portfolio. The material will answer the question of "How?" at the most practical level.

This strategy intends to be a general guideline but specific enough to be useful to anyone with the desire and patience to customize it to his or her own personal situation. Or, maybe even better, go through it with your financial advisor and charge them with helping you integrate it! This is obviously not the only way to go about charitable giving. What is important is that those who desire to invest in eternity develop *some* strategy to accomplish the goal.

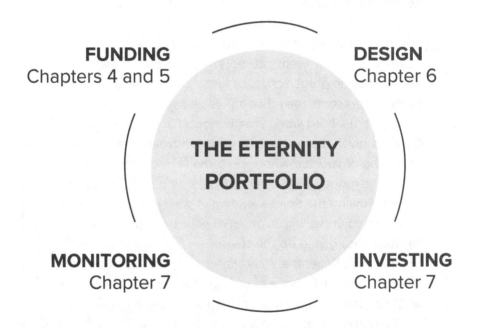

FUNDING
Chapters 4 and 5

DESIGN
Chapter 6

THE ETERNITY PORTFOLIO

MONITORING
Chapter 7

INVESTING
Chapter 7

FUNDING THE PORTFOLIO

We'll lay the financial groundwork and cover the question of "How much is enough?" from three distinct viewpoints. I'll address different methods of calculating annual giving and will introduce case studies to illustrate the process in action.

DESIGNING THE PORTFOLIO

Once you have established the funding for the portfolio, you have to plan how to give it away. The Eternity Portfolio is designed to be diversified across what I would identify as the major priorities listed in the Bible—evangelism, discipleship, and justice/mercy. Each of these major categories has subcategories. We will discuss how I came up with the categories, some ideas for determining what percentage of the portfolio should be allocated to each area, and when to consider "overweighting" a particular category.

INVESTING THE PORTFOLIO

Once you decide the categories,, the harder decisions begin. We have to make actual investment selections among the thousands of charities in existence, and we should not make these investments haphazardly. I'll recommend guidelines to help you find and screen appropriate candidates. This process combines prayer, the leading of the Holy Spirit, and God-given principles for effective ministry and accountability. The result is the faithful management of your Eternity Portfolio.

MONITORING AND ONGOING DUE DILIGENCE

A large part of success in any endeavor is formalizing goals, objectives, and guidelines in written form. Traditionally, an investment portfolio includes a written investment policy statement detailing how the portfolio will be managed. In much the same way, you may want to document the process for managing your Eternity Portfolio. We'll discuss the key ingredients of a successful policy statement, including the mission statement, funding strategy, investment selection, and due diligence requirements.

> Due diligence (and looking for new opportunities) has led me to no longer ask, "How much do I need to give," but "What should I give beyond my regular giving based on all I have left?"
>
> *Dr. Johnny Hunt*

PLANNING FOR THE FUTURE

Once you have your Eternity Portfolio functioning, you'll look to the future. We'll examine effective ways you can leave both a living legacy and a financial legacy, and we'll discuss specific techniques for advanced philanthropy. Finally, we'll look at the seven golden keys for honoring God and creating maximum leverage through our giving.

As we look once again at our investing equation, we have outlined the *vision* based on values and desire for rewards. In the chapters ahead, we'll add a *strategy* based on discipline and biblical wisdom—and we'll be on our way to successful investment.

THE ETERNITY PORTFOLIO

VISION		
VALUES	**GOALS**	**REWARDS**
Invest in others	Physical needs met	ETERNAL REWARDS
Physical needs	Good relationships	• Treasures in Heaven
Spiritual, emotional, and mental development	Spiritual vitality	• Crowns
	Productive people	• Positions of authority

STRATEGY		
DISCIPLINE	**Issues/Tools**	**WISDOM**
Planning	How much is enough?	Bible/Prayer/Holy Spirit
Communicating	Taxes	Advisors
Spending	Legacy	Experience
Saving	Due diligence	Books and other resources
	Investments	
	Giving strategy	
	Charitable trusts	

DISCUSSION QUESTIONS

1. Are you intentional about your responsibilities as a manager of God's resources? If not, why not?

2. What are some things that motivate you to give? Have you ever given with selfish motives?

3. In the past, how have you gone about deciding when to give, where to give, and how much to give? In what ways would you like to change that process?

4. During childhood, most of us learned about money either through the teaching or example of our parents. Which of these "money lessons" from your parents specifically related to giving have carried over into your adult years?

4

Funding the Portfolio: How Much Is Enough for Now?

- How much to give or how much to keep?
- Exponential generosity
- Determining how much is enough for now
- Ten thousand percent investment returns

One of my clients came to me while she was working for a successful technology company. As one of the company's first employees, her hard work had been rewarded with stock options that at one point were worth millions of dollars. Before coming to see me she had sold some of her stock to achieve a little investment diversification and had paid cash for her new home. But most of her assets were concentrated in the company stock. Then a stock market crash struck with all its fury. Especially hard hit were the technology companies, even those with solid businesses such as the one where my client worked. Over that period of months, the value of her stock and options fell by more than 75 percent.

When she came to me, we began to talk about the future and what amount of assets she would need to provide for her family's financial independence. She was dismayed to realize she had already passed that level *twice*, once on the way up and then again on the way down. I remember what she said to me because, unfortunately, I've heard it before: "Alan, if I had only come sooner, if I had only known *how much is enough*, I would have sold more stock and secured my family's financial independence."

It was not greed that kept this woman from achieving her goals but a lack of understanding of the finish line. In investing as well as life, understanding the end goal and knowing the right questions to ask can make or break your strategy.

When it comes to giving, your perspective drives the questions. If you consider giving primarily a duty, the question tends to be "*How much is enough giving* to fulfill my obligation and keep me from feeling guilty?" However, if you believe giving is really the ultimate investment, the question becomes "*How much is enough for me and my family* so I can maximize my giving?"

> The *most* important question in life is "Who do you say Jesus is?" and if we say He is my Savior and Lord, then we need to answer the second most important question, "How much is enough?" If we do not, then the desire for more of this world's goods will try to become lord.
>
> I knew we needed to answer this question when I owned my own broker/dealer financial services company. As the company grew, my wife and I realized we need to know how much is enough for us to live on now and how much is enough for retirement. Thank the Lord we answered that question about five years before we sold the company. When it sold it was worth way more than we had ever imagined. Therefore the "extra" (which by the way was more than we kept) was given away to God's work.
>
> I have always thought it was good we knew the answer to how much is enough before I knew the real value of the company or I might have put the number a little higher.
>
> *Lorne Jackson*

No matter how you calculate it, there is a fundamental, inverse relationship between how much you spend and how much you can give. In other words, more of one means less of the other. God has provided each of us with a certain amount of resources. Those resources, according to Scripture, are for two purposes: family and others. Once we have prayerfully determined how much we need to provide for family, the balance can be invested in others for the greater long-term reward.

HOW MUCH SHOULD I GIVE?

The starting line for building the Eternity Portfolio is funding. How much will you set aside this year to invest in others?

There are different methods for determining this amount. Most of us are familiar with the "tithe," or giving 10 percent of our gross income. Another method is to begin each year with a specific amount or percentage in mind as the target.

As long as the process integrates the biblical principles for giving (proper motives, systematic, proportionate, generous), there is no one "right" amount or method for everyone. However, as you consider how much you can give, think about the traditional investments you are making. How have you decided what you should invest there?

Take retirement savings, for instance. Retirement comes up in almost every financial-planning conversation. "How will this spending decision affect my retirement?" "Can we save a little more here or there to put more in retirement?" The list goes on and on. Typically, once someone understands the benefits of investing for retirement, he or she begins to look for opportunities to invest as much as possible.

Why is this particular investment so close to our hearts? Retirement is by far the most important and most long-term investment vision people have. It is the ultimate "end game" of earthly planning. To an extent, this is as it should be. As you get older, health and other issues can hamper your ability to work and earn a living. Wisely saving for the future is a characteristic of the faithful manager.

In the same way, once we realize the benefits of giving, we should be looking for every opportunity to invest in our Eternity Portfolio. The first step is to prayerfully and thoughtfully establish the funding requirements for our Family Portfolio. When we do that, we free up the balance for the investment with the greatest long-term potential—the Eternity Portfolio. We are then in a position to be used by God as a pipeline for His resources to bless others. I call this the "exponential generosity" method of funding.

Be forewarned: Exponential generosity is not for the timid or the faint of heart. It faces daily challenges from the thriving strains of the "keeping up with the Joneses" and "getting ahead in this world" viruses that constantly try to reassert themselves as financial priorities in our lives. Whether you're ready for this funding method depends largely on your vision of the rewards of investing.

EXPONENTIAL GENEROSITY

Exponential generosity is based on the supposition that at some level of financial blessing, it is no longer about me, and the future rewards from giving are far more valuable than the gratification of current spending. In other words, as God "overflows my cup" financially, I stop looking for a bigger cup and allow the blessings to flow to others.

> It's quite a challenge to sit from time to time and ponder this question: "How much would I have to *have* in order to *give* what I sense God wants me to give?
>
> *Dr. Johnny Hunt*

> I have observed that those who are always looking for a bigger cup never have enough, whereas those who let it overflow to others can't give it away fast enough. I walked into church one Sunday and met a member who is a very successful business-man. I asked how business was going, and he said, "My wife and I have been trying to give away more, and the more we give the more we find coming back in. We have been trying to outgive God, but we're learning that the more we give the more our business prospers. So we give away more. It is amazing."
>
> *Lorne Jackson*

> It is a radically different question to ask, "How much should I keep?" rather than "How much should I give?"
>
> *Todd Harper*

Wealth is not a bad thing, nor is enjoying some of that wealth wrong. Scripture says that God "gives us richly all things to enjoy" (1 Timothy 6:17). However, if I enjoy everything now, I forfeit my future rewards.

Exponential generosity divides your financial resources into the Family Portfolio and the Eternity Portfolio. It takes into account what you need to spend and save to provide for current and future family needs. The balance you can invest for all eternity.

Obviously each individual situation will be different. God has strategically placed Christians in all walks of life and at all economic levels. He knows exactly what financial resources you need to live the life He intends, and that level will probably not be the same for you as it is for others.

Fictitious case studies can provide practical examples for some of the concepts we discuss. Let's look now at one example of how exponential generosity might work.

Donna Rutherford is forty-seven years old and works for United Package Company in Minneapolis, Minnesota. Her current salary and bonus total $74,000 per year. Donna has been saving for retirement since she started work at age twenty-three, and she owns a nice home about thirty miles outside of Minneapolis. Donna has developed the funding schedule in this chart for her Eternity Portfolio; the table allows for a simple calculation of how much she plans to give each year.

Donna's current income is $74,000. Based on the table, she would give $2,500 on the first $25,000 (10 percent); $3,750 on the next $25,000 (15 percent); and then $6,000 on the remaining $24,000 (25 percent) for a total of $12,250 in giving for the year. Notice that her formula applies from the first dollar she earns.

Donna's family expenses and savings get $22,500 of the first $25,000 (90 percent); $21,250 of the next $25,000 (85 percent); and $18,000 of the remaining $24,000 (75 percent) for a total of $61,750. The results look something like this:

DONNA RUTHERFORD
EXPONENTIAL GENEROSITY

INCOME	GIVING PERCENTAGE
$0-25,000	10 %
$25,001-50,000	15 %
$50,001-100,000	25 %
$100,001-150,000	30 %
$150,001-up	50 %

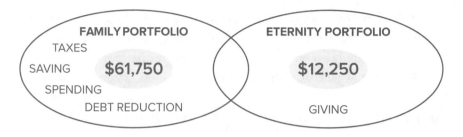

This is one example of a giving schedule. Appendix A details five case studies, and each family has a different funding calculation. These examples should give you some ideas regarding your own situation.

HOW IT WORKS

Before we discuss the obvious question of how to develop your own schedule, we should make some practical observations about how exponential generosity works.

First, this method of giving is *systematic*. We have not yet determined the "where" or "when" of our giving process, but the "how much" question is being answered. Donna has a portfolio of $12,250 she has determined proactively not to spend on herself but to invest for the benefit of others. Note that the plan does not exclude spontaneous giving. Certainly Donna will also have opportunities when she is led to give additional amounts, but the systematic plan serves as a foundation.

Second, this method is *proportionate* because, as Donna makes more money, she gives away a larger percentage of each additional dollar. This reflects the belief that as our needs are met, we can make a larger investment in meeting the needs of others. Donna has, in effect, set a limit on her living expenses. If you look again at her giving schedule you'll see that for income over $150,000, Donna will have only a small amount left to spend after giving and taxes.

Finally, exponential generosity *clarifies our money motives*. If we have a plan for giving away a large portion of any additional money we earn, our priorities are simplified. A balanced perspective for the kingdom of God, not greed, becomes the only motivation to make more money.

An interesting side benefit of exponential generosity is that over time you build in a significant "downside protection." If Donna loses her job or experiences a large cut in pay, she will be living so far within her means that the blow will be much less painful.

As I was researching the idea of exponential giving, it surprised me to find examples of people throughout history who used this very system to determine how much to give. Look at this example from the 1800s:

> Hence the propriety of a rule adopted by Mr. N. R. Cobb, a merchant of Boston: to give from the outset one quarter of the net profits of his business; should he ever be worth $20,000, to give one half of the net profits; if worth $30,000, to give three quarters; and if ever worth $50,000, to give all the profits. This resolution he kept till his death, at the age of 36, when he had already acquired $50,000, and was giving all his profits.[1]

This system has also been used in more recent times by men and women who want to maximize their investment in eternity. R. G. LeTourneau, a brilliant inventor and businessman of the twentieth century, gave away 90 percent of his earnings and lived on the balance. For more contemporary giving stories, check out www.GenerousGiving.org and read about people like Renee Lockey ("Work like a doctor, live like a nurse") and Alan Barnhart ("Where is your finish line?").

A proactive strategy is the best way to position yourself according to this passage in the Psalms: "If riches increase, do not set your heart on them" (62:10). There is a tremendous freedom that comes from knowing you are going to give away a larger and larger piece of that next dollar. You have not set your heart on it, so whether God will bring more wealth your way does not concern you anymore.

In order to develop a customized exponential generosity schedule, you need to answer two foundational questions:

1. How much is enough for *now?* (current living expenses)
2. How much is enough for *good?* (future living expenses)

Before you can answer these questions, it is important to have a good understanding of your current financial situation, including a cash-flow statement, balance sheet, and a list of your current insurance coverages. We'll describe the basic elements in the following pages.

HOW MUCH IS ENOUGH FOR NOW?

Start right where you are. Take out a piece of paper and list your income and expenses. Don't spend too much time trying to make it exact; just get a sense for the round numbers. Use a format similar to the annual cash-flow statement shown below. If you are the organized type, print out a cash-flow report from whatever system you use in order to set up your annual cash-flow statement. Notice that your current giving should be listed under "Investments (Eternity Portfolio)."

ANNUAL CASH FLOW STATEMENT

INCOME

Salary/bonuses	_____
Interest & dividends	_____
Retirement income	_____
Rents	_____
Business Income	_____
	_____
TOTAL INCOME	_____

EXPENSES

Mortgage/rent	_____
Property taxes	_____
Food	_____
Clothes	_____
Auto	_____
Recreation	_____
Income taxes	_____
Insurance	_____
	_____
TOTAL EXPENSES	_____

CASH FOR INVESTING | _____
(Income - Expenses)

INVESTMENTS

Eternity Portfolio	_____
Retirement plans	_____
Other investments	_____
College funds	_____
TOTAL INVESTMENTS	_____

EXCESS CASH FLOW | _____
(Cash for Investing - Total Investments)

The point of this exercise is to see how much you are currently invest-ing in all core areas of your finances, including your giving. This may take some time, but the result will probably be enlightening. If the "Cash for Investing" number is negative (in other words, if your current expenses are greater than your current income), you have another problem: You are liv-ing above your means. I suggest you immediately address this issue through prayer and godly counsel. Check with your local church to see if they have a financial-counseling ministry or can refer you to one. DaveRamsey.com as well as Crown.org have great resources on getting out of debt, budgeting, etc. While you work out the shortfall, I would still strongly recommend that you start your investment in the Eternity Portfolio. I have heard many stories of people in that exact situation who started giving and found their way out of the financial crisis much sooner than expected.

Let's look at some major items on the cash-flow worksheet. Each of these is a key element in your financial plan, and all of these elements together affect your giving strategy. If you're a faithful manager in all areas of your finances, you'll be able to be more deliberate in your giving.

RISK MANAGEMENT (INSURANCE)

One of the areas most often overlooked when it comes to reviewing cash flow is managing risk through insurance. This is probably because we have difficulty understanding the tangible benefits for the dollars spent. Until your house burns down or you have an automobile accident, you don't realize the value of insurance. And when it comes to life insurance, you only receive its value once you're dead! No wonder most people are underinsured.

From a purely financial stand-point, insurance is a cost-effective means of transferring the risk of catastrophic expenses to an insur-ance company. Proper financial

INSURANCE

PROPERTY AND CASUALTY
Home
Cars
Excess liability
Personal property
HEALTH
Accident/sickness
Long-term care
Life
INCOME
Disability

management requires appropriate insurance coverage. The table shows some of the areas you should review with an experienced insurance agent. Part of the reason most people avoid buying insurance is because they do not understand it and feel vulnerable to being taken advantage of. Educate yourself before making decisions in this area, but do not avoid the decision.

Adequate insurance coverage is foundational for the faithful manager. It lays the groundwork and protects the Family Portfolio against risks.

> Prudent risk management frees me up to be more generous rather than stockpiling for a "rainy day." I've embraced this idea in my life because I want to take good care of my family, but I don't want to emphasize capital accumulation to the detriment of my giving.
>
> *Todd Harper*

INCOME TAXES

The largest nondiscretionary expense you have is income tax. Without proper planning (and sometimes even with it) federal and state income taxes can consume *more than half* of the income you generate. Most people are not quite in that highest tax bracket, but when you include Social Security and Medicare taxes, the total could easily be 30 to 40 percent of your taxable income. Although Scripture is clear that we are obligated to pay our taxes, as faithful managers we are only obligated to pay the minimum required. This should be an area of particular attention in your planning, especially as it relates to your charitable giving. For those who itemize deductions on their tax returns, charitable giving is one of only a handful of truly tax-advantaged investments you can make. In the United States, each dollar you give to a qualified charity reduces your taxable income by a dollar.[2] As your taxable income goes down, your taxes go down. For example, if you are in the 15 percent income-tax bracket, you would save fifteen cents in taxes for each dollar you give. The government, in effect, pays 15 percent of your gift. Think of the savings if you are in a high tax bracket and your combined federal and state tax rate is 45 percent. Due to the tax savings, you actually pay only fifty-five cents on the dollar for each gift to charity!

The benefits can be even more attractive if you give away stock or other capital assets that have increased in value over the years. If you sell these, you will have to pay tax on the capital gains. However, if you give the appreciated assets, you do not pay tax on the gain, and, generally, neither does the charity.

> Example: Jeff Broward owns five hundred shares of Coca-Cola stock worth $20,000. He purchased these shares fifteen years ago for $2,000, so Jeff has what is called a "capital gain" of $18,000. He wants to make a contribution of $20,000 to his church. He could use cash, but he is considering gifting these shares. If he sells the shares for himself, the tax would be $3,600, so the cash value of the stock to Jeff is really $16,400 ($20,000 minus the $3,600 tax). Which should he give? Whether he gives cash or stock, the church gets $20,000. If he gives the cash, Jeff is left with stock worth $16,400 to him (due to the capital gain tax payable upon sale). If he gives the stock, he has $20,000 in cash left. Jeff gives the stock.

The opportunity to eliminate a capital gain and future tax down the road is pretty compelling. If you are considering this type of transaction, be sure to consult an experienced tax advisor to make sure all the details are executed properly. Incidentally, most large churches and ministries have brokerage accounts in place and can help facilitate this type of transaction.

> Consider contacting the National Christian Foundation to see how they can help get your gift of stock, property, real estate, or whatever else into a giving fund and out to your preferred organizations from there.
>
> *Heather Tuininga*

As you move into more advanced charitable-giving strategies, you need to take certain limitations into consideration. These rules limit the amount of income you can offset each year with charitable contributions. In general, you can deduct up to 50 percent of your income in any one year for gifts of cash to public charities. Contributions over that amount can be carried forward as deductions on future tax returns for up to five years.

> Example: Michelle Johnson earned $40,000 this year. She also received an inheritance of $35,000 upon the death of her grandmother. Michelle wants to make cash donations totaling $25,000 to her church and a homeless shelter in the area. Due to the income limitation, Michelle will be able to deduct $20,000 of her donations on her tax return this year ($40,000 income multiplied by 50 percent). The remaining $5,000 charitable contribution will be carried forward to her tax return next year.

One final note on the tax impact of investing in the Eternity Portfolio: *Taxes should not drive or control your investment strategy.* In the traditional investing arena, the overall after-tax economic result is what is important. Minimizing your taxes is not *the* goal but a means to the goal. As a faithful manager, you should not overlook the tax benefit of giving, and you should take steps to make optimal use of the tax system. However, there will be times when you should make gifts that are not tax deductible. It is the eternal reward that must be in view, not simply income-tax savings.

> My friends Don and Doris ask the question, "Who controls your giving?" the HS or the IRS (Holy Spirit or Internal Revenue Service). Do we quit giving when we go past the deductible thresholds? Are we willing to respond to God's prompting regardless of the tax implications?
>
> *Todd Harper*

OTHER LIVING EXPENSES

Lifestyle is a personal decision and calling. God has placed us in a specific moment at a specific place for a specific purpose. He does not have a "Christian standard of living" that is applied across the board. What one culture considers a necessity might be the height of luxury in another. Sacrifice is relative. We need to find the proper balance between living today and preparing for tomorrow (and that really long tomorrow!). I am reminded of Jesus' words to the disciples:

> And do not seek what you should eat or what you should drink, nor have an anxious mind. For all these things the nations of the world seek after, and your Father knows that you need these things. But seek the kingdom of God, and all these things shall be added to you. (Luke 12:29–31)

Our Father knows all the things we need, and He will provide. Our job is to be faithful managers and evaluate all spending decisions as spiritual decisions. You must make the final choice as to how you will allocate the money you receive. Remember: the money you spend on yourself is money you don't have available to give. *The challenge is to learn contentment so that at whatever place you are, you have enough.* I have been amazed to see in my own life and through consulting with my clients that spending almost always keeps up with income. Whether someone makes $20,000 or $2,000,000 per year, there is no shortage of creative ways to spend it.

This is a great opportunity for reflection and deeper study: what does the Bible say about lifestyle? About accumulating wealth?
David Wills

I filter lifestyle decisions with the question, "Am I more in love with the kingdom of God than with the kingdom of this world?" How does my money evidence that? I want to have as few idols as possible.

Jack Alexander

Lifestyle decisions start with separating needs and wants. The more giving I do, the less attractive lifestyle spending becomes. I think about the opportunity costs of spending a dollar versus investing it in God's kingdom. I consider, "How am I being salt and light, glorifying God through my lifestyle choices?

Larry Powell

We must learn contentment if we are going to maximize our investments, and one way to learn it is to limit the "spending" category by preprogrammed investing in other areas, be that for college, retirement, giving, short-term needs, or building up an emergency cash reserve.

Most of us have the opportunity to have a certain amount automatically deducted from our paychecks and invested in our retirement accounts. We do not consider that amount in our spending decisions because it is "off-limits." We need to do the same thing with our giving.

I heard it said years ago that, *"God will be a debtor to no man."* I know this to be absolutely true, however, it seems with each new year, my mind finds new ways to challenge divine results with human wisdom. May He give me the victory based on all His battles won.

Dr. Johnny Hunt

I recommend you start with the cash-flow statement and try to determine what level of spending is enough for now. Look ahead several years into the future and make some calculations. In the coming pages we will discuss in detail some of the issues surrounding your investments, but remember the goal: *Position yourself so God can channel His resources through you to be invested for maximum return in your Eternity Portfolio.*

After you set some limits on spending, the next question is where and how much to invest, for both the Family Portfolio and the Eternity Portfolio.

As you plan your approach for the future, I encourage you to invest at least 10 percent in your Eternity Portfolio. You may not be able to get to 10 percent at this point, but set that as an initial target. It gets much more interesting than that, but the important thing is to start *somewhere.*

> I do not believe one can settle how much we ought to give. . . . The only safe rule is to give more than we can spare. In other words, if our expenditure on comforts, luxuries, amusements, etc., is up to the standard common among those with the same income as our own, we are probably giving away too little. If our charities do not at all pinch or hamper us, I should say they are too small. There ought to be things we should like to do and cannot do because our charitable expenditures exclude them.
>
> —*C. S. Lewis, English author and scholar (1898-1963)*

INVESTING FOR RETIREMENT

The ultimate investment for the Family Portfolio is saving for retirement. It is only prudent during the prime working years to save money for the future, when earnings may be more limited. The issue then becomes balancing your retirement savings with other goals. How much should you be putting aside for retirement?

Each situation is different. A lot depends on how old you are, how much you have already saved, what type of work you do, and what it will cost to retire at the standard of living you choose. The irony is that even if you nail down all those factors, you still have no idea how the future will turn out. It may be that due to market conditions you end up with much more than you need (or much less). The cost of living can change dramatically over twenty to thirty years of retirement. Deteriorating health could make retirement much more expensive or much less (if you pass away earlier than expected). Some things are out of our control. Our faith will be tested even if we take all the wise steps necessary to prepare for retirement.

We must be careful, however, not to ignore other priorities in life by focusing solely on saving for retirement. Notice this in the parable Jesus taught about a certain rich man who seemed to be prepared:

> Then he said to them, "Watch out! Be on your guard against all kinds of greed; a man's life does not consist in the abundance of his possessions."
>
> And he told them this parable: "The ground of a certain rich man produced a good crop. He thought to himself, 'What shall I do? I have no place to store my crops.'
>
> "Then he said, 'This is what I'll do. I will tear down my barns and build bigger ones, and there I will store all my grain and my goods. And I'll say to myself, "You have plenty of good things laid up for many years. Take life easy; eat, drink and be merry."'
>
> "But God said to him, 'You fool! This very night your life will be demanded from you. Then who will get what you have prepared for yourself?'
>
> "This is how it will be with anyone who stores up things for himself but is not rich toward God." (Luke 12:15–21, NIV)

This teaching comes immediately before Jesus talks about how the Father will provide for all our needs and that we should focus on laying up treasure in heaven. Does this mean it is wrong to save for retirement? No. However, we must not focus so much on saving for retirement that we neglect other, more important areas of investing, such as our Eternity Portfolio. We are not guaranteed tomorrow, much less twenty years from now, so we need to be investing for several different goals and time horizons simultaneously.

So what does a balanced approach to investing look like?

We met Donna Rutherford earlier when discussing exponential generosity. Now let's look at her scheduled retirement savings. Donna is forty-seven, so she is investing 15 percent of her annual

DONNA RUTHERFORD
RETIREMENT FUNDING

AGES	INVEST
47-55	15 %
56-67	12 %

income for retirement. She is contributing the maximum amount possible to her company's 401(k) plan and then saving the balance in other investment accounts earmarked for retirement.

The case studies in Appendix A illustrate five different plans for systematically saving for retirement. None of them should be considered the "best" way. They are simply examples of how different people have taken a thoughtful approach to saving. For some helpful ideas, look for the one that comes closest to your particular situation.

In each case study, three critical factors significantly impact the results of retirement savings. First is the *systematic plan*. Year in and year out, money is being invested on a regular basis. Second is the *element of time*. When it comes to saving for retirement, time is either the savior or destroyer, depending on where you are in the process. At age twenty-five, the tolerance for error in your retirement program is quite high; assuming you get started, it is hard to mess up. However, once you hit age forty, that tolerance for error begins to narrow considerably. Over age fifty, you need to be putting the final touches on a well-executed plan. It is never too late to start, but you must have realistic expectations of what you can accomplish in a short amount of time.

The third major factor in investing for retirement is *achieving a certain level of growth over time*. In each of the case studies, the growth rate is assumed to average 6 percent annually. That 6 percent will not, however, come in a straight line. The average takes into account that there will be years of 5, 10, and 20 percent growth as well as years of 5, 10, and 20 percent *decline*, and everything in between.

We will discuss some basics of a successful retirement investment strategy in chapter 5, but for now, understand that you need consistent growth over time to maximize your retirement savings.

ENTREPRENEURS AND THE UNIQUE CHALLENGE OF CAPITAL ALLOCATION

Entrepreneurs have been uniquely gifted and motivated to transform capital (human, financial, material) into

Continued on next page

something greater than the sum of its parts. Entrepreneurs identify a need, see the opportunity, and then develop a solution—often identifying a need or desire that won't be understood by others until they're presented with the solution. Consider how few of us "needed" a smartphone until we experienced the power it would put in our pocket! Whether a business entrepreneur imports raw materials to fabricate into a smartphone, or a social entrepreneur integrates technology and human capital to create better outcomes in public schools, or a private equity investor evaluates investment proposals, those who allocate capital as their primary calling face unique challenges. Thinking specifically about financial capital, the entrepreneur must constantly evaluate how much to invest in growth and sustainability. Often this means taking the net income generated in any given year and "plowing it back in" for the future of the organization. This is why it is so unfortunate that much of our popular culture, including media, entertainment, and political forces, have demonized "profits" as somehow taking from others. In fact, having something at the bottom line—net income, profit, whatever the label—earned with integrity and Christian consideration for the needs of others, is essential to the long-term viability of most ventures. Existing commitments cost more over time, whether people (think pensions, healthcare, salary increases) or maintenance of physical plant, property, and equipment. Also, economic downturns and unforeseen difficulties arise requiring additional funds. The world is constantly changing and organizations must grow, invest in new directions, and adapt to survive. All these require either net income (including accumulations from prior years) or new money invested from outside,

Given these competing financial needs, how should a

thoughtful entrepreneur determine ways to invest in God's kingdom with an Eternity Portfolio mindset? First, you can deal with any salary you take in ways described throughout this book. Next, you have to prudently reserve for the needs of the organization—particularly thinking about future commitments to existing employees, maintenance of physical property, and some amount for unforeseen risks. Based on your experience in the business, also reserve some portion for ongoing adaptation, or research and development, to maintain position in the industry (note that this typically requires some base amount of growth). Then we get to the toughest decisions: investing for significant future growth and new endeavors. How do you think about doing that within your organization versus distributing the capital to traditional giving opportunities or even to other entrepreneurs? There is no simple decision matrix that fits everyone. Prayer, wisdom, and the advice of godly counselors and peers are all important to the process. As you develop a thinking methodology—and you will need a methodology because for most entrepreneurs, this isn't an event, it's a lifetime—I recommend you continuously circle back to two threshold questions: *Why, exactly, am I making this investment?* and *Is my control or influence getting in the way of God's best?*

Continuously asking why clarifies motives.
Why, exactly, am I making this investment? As you spend time in self-examination, you'll realize the answers to this seemingly simple question are many and complex. Is it because of pride? Desire to do more good in the world? Leadership peer pressure? Desire for more power? Boredom? Hope for a better future for my family? Greed

Continued on next page

for more money? Fear that I won't be associated with a dynamic, cutting-edge business? Desire to do more, greater things for God? For the entrepreneur, so much of identity is tied up in the organizations and results of your life's work, and God uses those hopes, dreams, and fears to motivate you to use your talents in the world. But for those of us who are leaders, we can be pretty good at strategic rationalization—for Christians, even spiritual rationalization—of almost any growth plan or investment. *You must constantly press on the why, and realize you are the easiest person in the world to fool about your own motives.* Then, in for-profit ventures, money can be a great clarifier of the question. We may say, "It's not about the money," but I've found that stripping out the money motive makes me much more thoughtful, introspective, and cautious about new investment opportunities. It's sad but true: we never get completely past the struggle. For ministry leaders, it's not often the money that pushes their entrepreneurial spirit. But bad motives come in many forms, including professional competitiveness with other ministries or excessive pride that "God wants us to change the world by doing _____." Honest evaluation of motives is an uncomfortable but important discipline.

Control can be a problem.
Is my control or influence getting in the way of God's best?
Leaders tend to be good at directing and managing things. And, more often than not, good leaders wind up as primary influencers, even when not directly in control. This is one of the ways God designed the system to work for human flourishing. However, the natural result can become a force of habit and brings a whole host of psychological motives for keeping that control. Two control pitfalls are particularly

insidious because they often contain elements of truth and can be justified based on our lifetime of experience. The first is pride: *I'm the one who can best direct this opportunity.* The second is lack of faith: *If I don't control this opportunity, it won't turn out right.* Highly capable entrepreneurs who want to integrate their faith and leadership must prayerfully sort this out.

Importantly, the process of giving doesn't eliminate the control issue. In fact, a statement I heard from a seasoned executive more than twenty years ago still carries a lot of weight: "The next best thing to having a lot of money is controlling a lot of money." Just giving away economic and legal benefits—through a charitable foundation or making a large grant, for example—still leaves us needing to consider the appropriate amount of control.

There are good reasons to limit your influence, especially bringing other voices to the table and training up new leaders. But limiting my influence has, for me, become an issue of faith and curiosity. I want to see God evident more and more in daily life, and I'm curious as to how He will work things out. Often that means I have to get out of the way! Proactively removing myself from control positions has become a fun but challenging exercise. Note: you may find it more difficult to reduce your influence than you might imagine.

Look for ways to test your motives and build defenses against bad thinking. Intentional giving is one way to keep pressure on your financial motives. Also, consider how you might change your organizational structure to improve decision making and remove temptations lurking under the surface.

For decades, CEO Alan Barnhart and his brother Eric have operated their successful Memphis business, Barnhart

Continued on next page

Crane and Rigging, on an unusual set of principles. From their earliest days in business, the Barnhart brothers wanted to be about God's business and were concerned about the potential effects of money on their spiritual lives and their families. They decided to cap their salaries at the level of a middle-class, Memphis lifestyle and give away the profits not needed for growth. Eventually, they transferred 99 percent of the legal ownership through an arrangement with the National Christian Foundation. Profits from the company go to charitable causes all over the world, administered by a large committee of employees.

How might this amazing corporate giving structure affect business decisions at this fast-growing company? A quick look at the website (www.barnhartcrane.com) shows an organization "providing innovative solutions to complex lifting and transportation challenges faced by heavy industry," with locations in thirty-nine U.S. cities. The Barnhart company is not only working to grow organically, it is actively acquiring other companies.

Consider how the company makes growth investment decisions. As CEO, Alan Barnhart is motivated to provide a valuable service to customers, a productive and challenging work environment for employees, and growing resources to invest in God's kingdom. The company invests those resources inside the business, throughout the communities where it operates, and beyond to global charitable organizations. From a financial standpoint, the company invests 50 percent of net income in the growth of the organization and 50 percent through the giving strategy. The Barnharts have removed two of the main temptations that work against entrepreneurs—greed and control. More of the Barnhart story can be found in a video online at www.GenerousGiving.org.

Entrepreneurs are wired to transform capital into new, productive, creative forms. Those natural gifts carry tendencies that make it seductively easy to rationalize empire building and controlling behavior. The regular discipline of self-examination—in light of Scripture and in a spirit of prayerful, humble, intellectual honesty—can make all the difference. Then, consider financial and structural boundaries that act as guardrails for carrying out that God-given mission while simultaneously investing in kingdom work beyond yourself.

There is a lot of godly kingdom-building that can come through an entrepreneur investing in his business. But we have to avoid the trap of assuming we can compound capital faster than God. If He wants us to give elsewhere, we can be assured the kingdom compounding will be even greater.

Larry Powell

INVESTING FOR COLLEGE

At one time a college education was considered a *luxury* few could afford. Today higher education is a *necessity* few can afford. Tuition and related costs continue to rise even as new and revolutionary methods of saving for college sprout up on an almost annual basis. Fortunately there are a growing number of federal and state scholarship plans available to offset some of these costs. However, college funding remains a significant challenge for both parents and students.

We need to clarify priorities. Saving for college is not nearly the same priority level as saving for retirement. Providing a four-year degree for your children, while important, is not as important as making sure you don't have to move in with them when you turn sixty-five because your retirement funds run out! Keep in mind that college is not out of reach for those without the financial backing of their parents. Scholarships, loans, grants, work studies—the list goes on and on, but the point is that college is accessible even for those who must pay some or all of their own way.

If you have significant financial resources, you can estimate and set aside the amount you need to save for college rather easily. This information is widely available on websites such as www.savingforcollege.com. You can look at the average costs for different types of schools (for example, public, private, or elite) and plug in details such as the number of years until your children start college, the amount of savings you already have, and how much you are setting aside each month. This online calculator will increase the tuition cost for inflation each year until your children start college and then give you the amount you need to have set aside by the time they get there. It will also take the present value of that total, assuming a certain growth rate, and show you what you need to invest today.

The problem for most people is that, depending on how many children they have and where they will go to school, that amount can be simply out of reach. In college funding, as in retirement savings, we need balance and we need to face the realities of what we can accomplish.

In Case Study 2, John and Sheila Patterson's college plan is simple but effective. They have two children, ages six and four. John and Sheila have a combined income of $58,000 this year and are investing 4 percent each year toward their children's college education. They recognize that the kids will probably need some additional assistance through financial aid, jobs, and so forth, but John and Sheila feel that 4 percent achieves a balance in the family's priorities.

Contrast this with Todd and Emily Fleming in Case Study 3. Through the sale of their business, they were able to invest a lump sum of $275,000 for college funding.

Once you decide how much to invest for college savings, you then choose between the many different investment plans. Savingforcollege.com gives the pros and cons of the alternatives, including everything from savings bonds to the newer "529 plans." These 529 plans have become the college savings vehicle of choice because they allow large and small contributions, tax-free investment earnings, and the flexibility to change beneficiaries as needed. Also, you can use 529 plans at any accredited college (including Christian colleges and universities).

Educating your children is a priority. How you pay for it, especially at the college level and beyond, is a personal decision and should be guided by your economic situation. The earlier you begin to plan and save, however, the more options you will have.

INVESTING IN THE ETERNITY PORTFOLIO

Now we come to the annual investment in the Eternity Portfolio. This is the amount set aside each year for your giving strategy. As a baseline measurement, we will start this investment at 10 percent of total income. We then need to determine both when and how much we can increase our giving.

First we need to get an idea of where this additional investment comes from. Let's assume you are saving 15 percent of your annual income for retirement, 6 percent for your children or grandchildren's education, and 10 percent for your Eternity Portfolio. (For purposes of this comparison, income taxes are included with living expenses.) Depending on your annual income, the chart below shows the percentage invested by category:

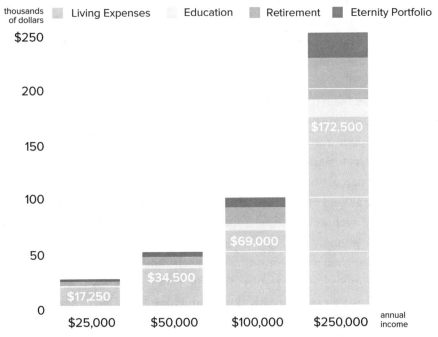

PERCENTAGE INVESTING

You invest the same amount of investment, from a percentage stand-point, at each income level (a total of 31 percent, including funds for retirement, college, and the Eternity Portfolio). Note that even though you invest the same percentages in each category at each income level, the absolute dollar amount left over for living expenses increases substantially as income increases.

By setting in place a tiered exponential-generosity schedule, we can allow for some increase in living expenses as needed while contributing a greater percentage of each additional dollar earned. As an example, remember the giving schedule for Donna Rutherford:

You may never reach the income levels shown on this schedule, but make up one that fits your particular situation. The key is to figure out where you will be able to level off your living expenses so giving can increase. As you make this decision, seek the Lord's leading. His guidance is essential if we are to follow His will in our giving.

ETERNITY PORTFOLIO
INVESTMENT SCHEDULE

INCOME	GIVING PERCENTAGE
$0-25,000	10 %
$25,001-50,000	15 %
$50,001-100,000	25 %
$100,001-150,000	30 %
$150,001-up	50 %

Don't be surprised if you start having more to give than you ever expected. The chart on the next page shows how Donna's giving schedule operates at the various income levels.

Do you see the difference? As the overall income increases, living expenses start to flatten out and giving increases exponentially. As opposed to a flat 10 percent of income, Donna is investing a growing *percentage* of her income as God provides it. Also, once she achieves shorter-term investment goals, such as education funding, there will be additional amounts freed up for giving.

As you might imagine, investing with a schedule like this creates the potential for enormous lifetime results. Take the Patterson family (Case Study 2). John and Sheila are in their early thirties and have established a similar tiered giving schedule for their Eternity Portfolio. Their combined annual income

EXPONENTIAL INVESTING

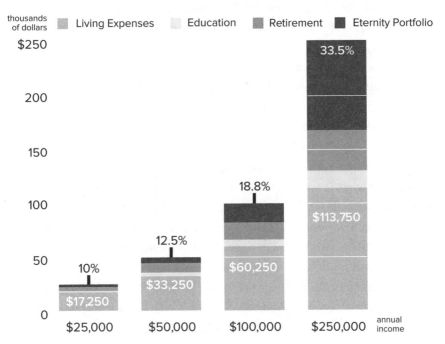

is $58,000. This year the Pattersons will give a little over $6,000. They will also contribute $2,000 or so for their children's education funds and invest 10 percent of their income for retirement. John and Sheila expect their income to increase modestly for inflation over the coming years.

How much can the Pattersons invest for eternity over their lifetimes? Can they really make a difference? The answer is a resounding *yes*. Projecting into the future, they will invest more than *one million dollars* in God's kingdom during their lifetime! This is a staggering figure and shows the difference it can make to have a strategy and apply it consistently over time.

Think of the needs this money will meet. Feeding the hungry, spreading the good news, teaching and discipling people around the world—all through the investment of one couple. Starting early and giving consistently as God blesses them with increase, John and Sheila will give away more than they keep for themselves. At the same time, they are providing for current living expenses as well as saving for education and for their own retirement.

But what about investment returns? If we are laying up treasure in heaven, our investments will compound over all eternity. Remember the words of Jesus when He talked about the rewards of making sacrifices and following Him?

> Everyone who has left houses or brothers or sisters or father or mother or wife or children or lands, for My name's sake, *shall receive a hundredfold, and inherit eternal life.* (Matthew 19:29, emphasis added)

Wow! What does "a hundredfold" look like? Setting aside annual compounding, what if we just received rewards equal to one hundred times what we invested? So, for example, if we invested $20,000 for eternity over our lifetime, a hundredfold return on investment would grow that number to $2,000,000. That's 10,000 percent in investment returns!

That little dark strip at the bottom of the chart below is the actual amount invested. Do you get a sense for the magnitude here? Ten thousand percent is a lot of growth. And this chart only covers the Pattersons' *lifetime.*

Okay, I realize that Jesus was speaking symbolically. We may not have this gigantic pile of rewards in heaven. Chances are the eternal rewards we

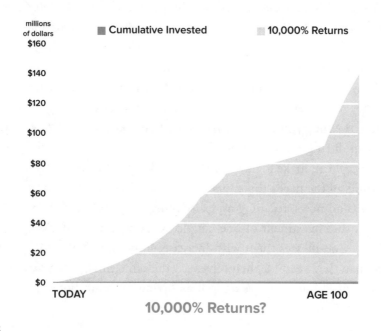

receive will be vastly different from anything we can imagine. However, even speaking symbolically, it still sounds like the rewards will be incredible and will be exponentially more than our investment in God's kingdom while we are here on earth.

GENEROSITY AS A WAY OF LIFE: Dr. Johnny Hunt

True generosity spreads beyond a relationship with money to every aspect of life. As God develops us in response to grace, we become increasingly generous with our time, relationships, social capital, and more. My pastor for almost twenty years, Dr. Johnny Hunt has been a close friend and role model in many ways, but particularly through his authentic, comprehensive life of generosity.

Growing up in government housing in North Carolina as one of six children raised by a single mom, Johnny Hunt was an unlikely candidate to eventually lead the largest protestant denomination in America. In fact, as a teenage alcoholic who dropped out of high school from fear of presenting an oral book report, he seemed unlikely to lead much of anything. But God had big plans for Johnny. One snowy Sunday evening at age twenty, he found himself in a church service instead of racing cars at the local dragstrip. He gave his life to Jesus—and everything changed. Even that first night, a flame of generosity began to burn as Johnny volunteered to clear the snow off car windshields in the church parking lot. The generosity of the kingdom shaped his early Christian life, with mentors teaching and leading by example. Paying for college and seminary. Assisting with expenses for his young family. Buying suits for the young pastor. Ordinary people would be the generosity heroes of those early days as God was laying the foundation. Decades later when Pastor Johnny was well

Continued on next page

beyond need, he visited one of these benefactors, a man named Odus Scroggs, on his deathbed at the hospital. This friend was so accustomed to God leading him to proactively give money that when he recognized Pastor Johnny, despite his state of semiconsciousness, he instinctively reached toward his back pocket to pull out his wallet!

Pastor Johnny became a bright light of God's grace, motivated by zeal for evangelism and fueled by a heart of generosity. Growing the church both locally (from a couple hundred to more than ten thousand in monthly attendance at First Baptist Church of Woodstock, Georgia, where he has pastored for almost thirty years) and globally (through church planting and mission efforts). Financially, Pastor Johnny has invested in hundreds of organizations (and countless individuals) outside the church, but I know him to be one of the largest givers *to our church*. Maybe that is why when Johnny speaks about the kingdom of God before taking the offering each Sunday, I often find it the most spiritually inspiring part of the entire service. People respond because he has the spiritual and moral authority of authentic, radical generosity. We are investing *together* in the kingdom.

But to those who know him well, the financial side isn't even the heart of Johnny's generosity. His generosity is relational. It's the thousands of phone calls, texts, and e-mails he responds to every month from people who need encouragement. It's the countless hours before and after speaking events he spends talking with struggling people who often need just a caring, empathetic ear. It's the organizations he has started to provide teaching, meet needs, and encourage people across a broad spectrum. It's Johnny and Janet hosting hundreds of guests at their home continuously throughout the year.

Pastor Johnny is serious about investing financially in

his Eternity Portfolio. I've heard him say that the Eternity Portfolio concept inspired him to be even more strategic in his giving as we collaborated on early drafts of the first edition. So the money is important. However, it is just one facet of a truly generous life.

TIME TO GET STARTED

I hope this chapter has helped you start thinking about your annual investment in the Eternity Portfolio. The point is to have a systematic way of deciding how much to invest, just as you would with any traditional investment. Throughout the process you should focus on *hearing from God* as to the amount and timing of your investment in the Eternity Portfolio. Diligent, intentional planning honors God but should never be a substitute for prayer and seeking His will for your giving.

A friend of mine named Steve, who works for the Coca-Cola Company, once told me how God had impressed on him the idea of paying off his home so he and his family could be in a position to give away the amount of their mortgage payment each month. After an extended time of prayer and studying the Bible, Steve and his wife sold their Coca-Cola stock and paid off the mortgage. This was back in 1998, just as the price of Coke stock was reaching its all-time high. Shortly after, the stock price dropped over 40 percent! Thanks to God's timing, Steve sold his stock at the peak, paid off their mortgage, and has had the freedom to invest many thousands of dollars in his Eternity Portfolio ever since.

Will something like that happen to you? Maybe not exactly, but you'll want to seek God's direction as it relates to the amount and timing of your giving.

Let's return to one other question posed at the beginning of the chapter. Will there come a time in your life when all other investment goals (including financial independence) have been accomplished? What then? Is that the time you can begin to focus even more on your eternal investments? More people than ever before are facing the question "How much is enough *for good?*" We'll take a look at this question in the next chapter.

DISCUSSION QUESTIONS

1. Do you have a financial plan for your Family Portfolio? Based on the information in this chapter, how faithful do you think you are being with your money in this area?

2. Have you ever considered the idea of establishing a limit on your family's expenses over time? What would be some of the benefits of such a limit? What would be the downside?

3. Based on your current budget or the annual cash-flow statement, what percentage of your current income have you scheduled to invest in your Eternity Portfolio?

4. Do you expect your income to increase, decrease, or stay the same over the next ten years? Who controls that?

5. How do you plan to be more intentional about your investment in the Eternity Portfolio over the next ten years?

6. How could you take greater advantage of the tax-savings opportunities in your giving (e.g., gifts of appreciated stock)?

5

Funding the Portfolio: How Much Is Enough for Good?

■ The importance of financial finish lines
■ What is financial independence for Christians?
■ Calculating "How much is enough?"
■ What happens if I cross the finish line?

The concept of *enough* is a challenging one. Godly wisdom teaches us to work hard, live beneath our means, and save for the future. Some of us have been going down that path for so long that it becomes simply habit to keep on putting money into savings and retirement accounts. And of course, once you have assets, it's natural to focus on growing, preserving, and protecting those assets from the various risks of the future. Who knows what will happen ten or twenty years down the road? Combine the global calamity reported daily on the Internet and evening news with the life insurance commercials, and how can we ever feel truly secure? Too often, those of us who have the most learned to keep hanging on tightly—usually in the name of prudence. Taken beyond a certain point, this "cocooning" process may cause us to miss out on God's best. What if we have "over-accumulated" beyond any reasonable measure of future living needs and don't realize it? What if we could take our Eternity Portfolio investing to a whole new level? Somehow we must balance godly wisdom and godly faith when it comes to our financial future. More Christians than ever before in history have to be thinking prayerfully about finish lines.

WHY SET A FINISH LINE?
By "finish line," I am referring not to the end of life, but to the end of your need to invest in your Family Portfolio (which, remember, includes retirement and college savings). There are three important reasons for identifying the financial finish line in your own life.

1. Setting the finish line makes it real.

Studies show you have a much higher probability of achieving goals that are specific and formalized in writing. Once you zero in on the bull's-eye, you actually have a chance of hitting it.

2. Finish lines keep you from taking unnecessary risks.

Remember my client from the beginning of chapter 4 who kept the bulk of her assets concentrated in one company's stock because she didn't realize she had crossed the finish line? Unfortunately, hers is not the only example I could give of someone who took extraordinary risks trying to reach a goal he or she had already achieved.

3. Finish lines allow you to redirect assets to more strategic opportunities.

Consider a goal like saving for college. People generally realize when they have accomplished this goal,, and then they shift their investment dollars to something else. Why? Because it makes no sense to keep piling up money for a goal you have already achieved if there are other, more compelling opportunities.

The same can be said of the big finish line: retirement savings. There are a growing number of people who have passed this line and kept saving. For what? Most of the time 50 percent of what's left goes to the government (in estate taxes) and 50 percent to the children. It is good to leave an inheritance for your children, but that goal can be quantified and surpassed as well, and it doesn't compare to eternal investment returns. Once you know and have reached the finish line, you can set your sights firmly on more strategic investment opportunities.

> I have a personal goal in light of the finish line: to give back to my church all that I have ever been paid. I heard Dr. W. A. Criswell tell how this became a reality for him. If this happens, or if I get close, my prayer is that my motive remains pure in giving to God's glory.
>
> *Dr. Johnny Hunt*

WHAT IS *FINANCIAL INDEPENDENCE?*

Financial independence is that place in time when you have enough. Taking into account pensions, Social Security, and other investments, this is when, by all prudent measures, you no longer need to earn a living. It is often synonymous with retirement because historically they were one and the same for most people.

Let me be clear that financial independence is not necessarily when you take up golf or gardening as a full-time occupation. It does not always mean you quit working. People today are beginning to realize that some of their most productive years come *after* they stop "making a living" and start "making a life" by doing something they are passionate about. Often this is only possible after many years of financial preparation.

For Christians, the term *financial independence* may have some negative connotations because we believe our dependence should always be on God, not on our financial resources. I am in no way saying you can reach a point where your financial future is secure apart from dependence on God. He ultimately controls the distribution and maintenance of all earthly wealth. However, as part of our faithful management of wealth, there may come a time when we change our overall investment strategy to focus more on our Eternity Portfolio instead of our Family Portfolio. We are instructed to save and prepare for the future and to support our families. However, at some point we may say we have accumulated enough in the Family Portfolio to last the rest of our lives. This is not an exact science, but it's an effort to determine how much more each of us can put to kingdom uses during our lifetime.

WHAT IF I NEVER GET TO THE FINISH LINE?

Most of us will always have part of our investments going into retirement accounts during our working years, and many will never have the perceived security of a sizable monthly pension or a large investment account. For them, the "finish line" calculations we will run later in this chapter may yield an insurmountable number. What to do then?

There are some obvious steps you can take to reach the finish line, such as extending your working years or cutting back on living expenses. But at the same time, continue investing in your retirement funds *and* continue investing in others through your Eternity Portfolio. We do not know what the future holds, but our heavenly Father does. He knows our needs and He has promised to provide for them. Remember that, in any event, retirement is still a very short-term goal when compared to eternity.

> For business owners, there can be a tendency to wait for a liquidity event and not realize there has been a competition for capital all along the way. There is an opportunity cost to delaying an investment in God's kingdom.
>
> *Larry Powell*

There are, however, a growing number of people who actually will come to a point where they do not need to add any more to the nest egg. They have crossed the finish line—a good many of them without knowing it. I am convinced that the reason they passed the finish line and kept going is twofold: First, they do not have a vision for the rewards of increasing their ultimate investment, the Eternity Portfolio. In other words, for many people, there *is* nothing better to do with their money, so they continue to accumulate. Second, it is difficult to quantify and understand the finish line for financial independence. And uncertainty brings anxiety. Where do you even *start* in trying to calculate a number?

HOW MUCH IS ENOUGH FOR GOOD?

At one time in America, life was simple for those who lived to be retirees. You worked thirty-five to forty years for one company, and that company agreed to pay you a nice pension starting at age sixty-five and lasting the rest of your life. The average life expectancy for people at that time was somewhere in the early seventies, so investing and inflation were not really much of a concern for the five to ten years of an average retirement. More people lived within their means since credit was not nearly as prolific in the culture.

Much has changed in the last thirty years. Today the average employee works at several different companies through the years, few of which even have pension plans. Life expectancies have increased, as have expectations of retired life. Gone are the days of retiring to the rocking chair on the porch. Today, many retirees will spend significantly more money in retirement than they did during their prime working years.

At least three distinct groups of people are preparing for retirement today. The first group is the last wave of the "pensioners." These folks are in their sixties and are finishing their long careers at older corporations or government agencies that still provide a meaningful monthly pension benefit. They tend to live within their means, which bodes extremely well for flexibility during their retirement years.

The group at the other end of the spectrum is what I will call the "opportunists," ranging in age from the early twenties to the early forties. None of the opportunists ever seriously believed they would get a pension from a company, and they're probably right. From their earliest working days, the investment mantra has been ringing in their ears, and the smart ones signed up for the maximum 401(k) deferral their first day on the job. They tend to change jobs *as the opportunity presents itself*, and they have understood from day one that whatever they save for retirement is all there is.

The last group is probably in the trickiest position. I'll call them the "transitioners" because they are right in the middle of a monumental change in how retirement is funded. This group tends to be older than forty-five. When the transitioners started their careers, the promise of a pension was still alive. Then corporate America changed, streamlining operations with technology more each year and revamping retirement plans to save costs. Layoffs and restructurings are now part of the standard operating procedure every few years. Even government has been forced to scale back—particularly at the state and local level. The result for many of these people is that their standard of living is based on a compensation package (salary and bonus) much higher than whatever pension (if any) they will receive in retirement. While many of them have sizeable retirement accounts, most have no idea how much money will be required (with investment discipline) to fund a given lifestyle over thirty years of retirement. As a simple example, it takes $1,000,000 in a properly invested retirement account to conservatively sustain $40,000 of annual retirement cash flow.

Each of these three groups faces significant challenges when planning for financial independence. First, their income will likely be some combination of pension, government benefits, and investment assets. Second, expenses will vary widely with changes in lifestyle, health, and inflation over the coming years. With all the variables, how can we possibly come up with a definitive measure of the finish line?

Remember, the point is not precision but general direction. There are numerous ways to estimate a ballpark number for how much money you'll need in retirement, but all of them involve these four factors:

1. **Cash-Flow Shortfall.** Assume you are retiring today. You expect to draw a pension of $45,000 and Social Security benefits of $11,000 per year, giving you a total annual income of $56,000. (For now, count only "regular" sources of retirement income, not including your investment assets.) After you spend some time reviewing expenses, it becomes obvious that you will need at least $72,000 per year, including taxes, to maintain your current standard of living. Your expenses outweigh your income by $16,000 ($56,000 income minus $72,000 expenses), and that's the amount of your annual shortfall.

How will you meet this shortfall? Maybe you decide to take on some part-time work. You could always look for places to cut back on expenses, or you could use your accumulated investment assets (which we'll discuss later). In any event, you'll need $16,000 per year to meet the expected shortfall.

If you do this exercise and have no cash-flow shortfall, you have achieved the finish line of financial independence!

The rest of this discussion is of no consequence to you except to the extent that inflation might catch up with a fixed retirement income.

2. **Life Expectancy.** Once you know your annual shortfall ($16,000 in our earlier example), the next step is determining your life expectancy. How many years will you need to fund the $16,000 shortfall in living expenses? We can only guess at life expectancy, so we should be conservative. (In retirement planning, it is more conservative to plan as if you will live longer.) The average tends to be in the late seventies, but

don't plan your retirement based on that. If you are married and you and your spouse are both in reasonably good health, there is a good chance at least one of you will make it into your eighties and maybe even beyond. I would recommend using the number of years until age one hundred to provide a conservative estimate.

3. Inflation. Do you ever stop to think how the price of things you buy has increased dramatically over the decades? Consider movie tickets or postage stamps. How many times has the price of these items doubled in the last thirty years? In a similar way, you should expect the cost of living to increase substantially over the period of your retirement. A good guess is probably 3 percent per year for most items and 8 percent per year for health-related expenses.

4. Investment Returns. Those with any experience investing money understand how difficult it is to predict investment returns for one year, much less over a twenty-to-thirty-year retirement. Be conservative. Throughout most of the last century, a diversified portfolio consisting entirely of stocks has returned approximately 10 percent per year. But remember, that is not 10 percent year-in and year-out. There are a lot of negative years that tend to even out the euphoria. My experience is that most people approaching retirement are not comfortable having their entire portfolio in the stock market. Also, once in retirement, you'll likely need fixed-income investments and cash to provide for annual withdrawals. So use a conservative number for your long-term portfolio growth-rate assumption, maybe 6 percent.

How do these four factors come together in helping you set a goal for financial independence? In our example, there is an annual cash shortfall of $16,000. The question is, how much money must I save and invest (at 6 percent annual growth) to be able to withdraw $16,000 per year (adjusted for inflation) for as long as my spouse and I are alive? Whether your annual cash-flow need is $16,000 or $1,000,000 per year, the math is essentially the same.

AFTER THE GREAT RECESSION

Many investors interested in the principles of the Eternity Portfolio have wondered if the old investment principles still apply today, in the wake of the Great Recession of 2008–2009 and ongoing sluggish global growth. "Hasn't the world changed for the worse?" Certainly we are dealing with problems that *have become more obvious and in many ways, progressively worse* since the Great Recession. Global indebtedness, the end of rapid Chinese economic growth, demographic aging, and the unraveling of the eighty-year European socialist experiment—what I call the Big Four profound economic changes—will reshape our world over the coming decades. Adapting to those major shifts will create volatility, asset bubbles, and societal pain (not least because politicians will work so hard to "fix things," spawning unpredictable, unintended consequences). But adapting will also bring about opportunity. God created us in His image, and that means we create things and we fix things. Nothing on the horizon indicates a change in His nature, and I expect the future to be full of innovation, social solutions, and life-changing technologies that are unimaginable today—all because people were created in His image.

The original Eternity Portfolio was written in the aftermath of 9/11 and the dot.com implosion—certainly not a time of bullish enthusiasm for the economy or financial markets. So its principles are meant to be timeless.

But I do believe this season in history portends slower economic growth (particularly outside the United States) and a higher probability of increasing armed conflict. So how does that affect our planning? First, remember that these problems have always been with us. *Investment returns accrue to disciplined savers in spite of and often because of the problems in the world.* Risk and uncertainty are the normal state, and our financial plans should assume them. Second, uncertainty is why we diversify across asset classes, geographies, and companies. Third, for planning purposes, the current state of the world is good reason to save more and lower your expected returns slightly. For example, in our fictitious examples, I've reduced our assumed investment return to 6 percent as opposed to the 7 percent we might have used ten or twenty years ago. That will still require a portfolio with a large allocation to diversified equity-type investments (stocks, real estate, private businesses, etc).

Also note I said, "for planning purposes." Remember our planning is just a baseline to understand the best human wisdom. It does not prevent us following the Holy Spirit in a different direction through our giving, career, and business decisions. No matter the economic environment, our hope and provision come from God alone. With discipline and wisdom as we pursue His calling—including a focus on our Eternity Portfolio—we can trust He will provide for our needs.

THE CAPITALIZATION APPROACH

A simple but effective way of getting a general idea of your finish line is called the *capitalization approach.* This method "capitalizes" your cash-flow shortfall into an investment goal. It is a simplified method of taking an annual cash shortfall and determining a rough estimate of how much you will need to set aside for your entire retirement. Once you have accumulated investment assets equal to the capitalized goal, you have achieved your finish line.

Use the capitalization approach worksheet that follows to make a rough calculation of your personal financial-independence finish line. Our example is based on a conservative capitalization rate of 25 times your cash-flow shortfall.

Although it may sound simplistic, there is a great degree of complexity woven into the magical "25 times" capitalization rate. Where does this come from?

Let's say a sixty-year-old woman needs $16,000 per year for every year of her retirement. If we assess her life expectancy at one hundred, she will need assets to cover forty years of retirement. Forty times $16,000 equals $640,000. However, because her invested assets will grow over the forty years, she doesn't really need as much as $640,000 right now. On the other hand, because of inflation, the cost of living will increase every year and she will need more than $16,000 annually. Given all these variables, how do we determine the right "finish line"?

As a conservative rule of thumb, I like to plan for an individual to withdraw no more than 4 percent of his or her retirement assets annually. Why 4 percent? Because if we estimate that the investments grow at least 6 percent annually, the return should offset inflation and most of the withdrawal. We can't count on that 6 percent return every year, as there will be good years and bad. However, based on history and a properly diversified portfolio, there is a low probability of an individual running out of money with a 4 percent withdrawal rate. So if 4 percent is our target withdrawal rate, we can determine how much is needed in savings for any amount of annual shortfall by multiplying the shortfall by 25 (the inverse of 4 percent).

In our example, to get our capitalized goal we would multiply our $16,000 shortfall by 25, giving us a finish line of $400,000. What exactly does that mean? The $400,000 represents a conservative estimate of what you would want to have invested in retirement savings in order to draw 4 percent annually ($16,000 in the first year) for the remainder of your lifetime. Because you are using a percentage, the actual withdrawal would be adjusted each year. In other words, as the account grows over time, your withdrawal grows as well to keep up with inflation.

Four hundred thousand dollars may sound like a huge number to yield only $16,000 per year in cash flow. In some ways that is true. For example, if you calculated an exact finish line based on achieving 6 percent returns *every year* for exactly forty years, the investment needed would be more like $260,000. The problem with this smaller goal is that it is much more likely to be used up prematurely given the variability of investment returns, the uncertainty about life expectancy, and the rising cost of living.

In other words, if everything works out exactly as planned, you can get by on less. But I don't recommend it. In general, you should plan to continue earning money from outside sources until your investments can prudently support the withdrawal rate. On the other hand, the $400,000 will likely provide some inheritance for your children or a bequest to charity upon your death. Obviously if you start with an assumption that your investments will earn substantially more than 6 percent over time, you will be able to withdraw more (or save less) to accomplish the same purpose.

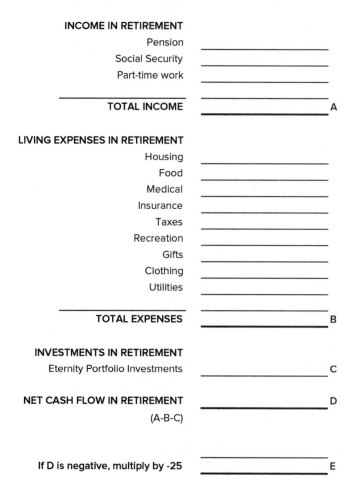

CAPITALIZATION APPROACH

Investment assets needed for financial independence

INCOME IN RETIREMENT

Pension

Social Security

Part-time work

TOTAL INCOME   A

LIVING EXPENSES IN RETIREMENT

Housing

Food

Medical

Insurance

Taxes

Recreation

Gifts

Clothing

Utilities

TOTAL EXPENSES   B

INVESTMENTS IN RETIREMENT

Eternity Portfolio Investments   C

NET CASH FLOW IN RETIREMENT   D

(A-B-C)

If D is negative, multiply by -25   E

> In the Great Recession, the Federal Reserve adopted a "zero interest rate policy," or ZIRP, which benefited people in debt while punishing savers. This has made it much more difficult to generate and project income to determine whether one's future needs can be covered.
>
> *Jack Alexander*

Your financial-independence finish line is only an estimate. It is useful to determine whether or not you are on the right track with your retirement savings. For some, this will be a wake-up call to invest in retirement. For others, however, this calculation will show that you have no cash short-fall—in fact, that you long ago passed the finish line. That is when you must give serious thought to the more strategic investment opportunities of the Eternity Portfolio.

WHAT HAPPENS AFTER I CROSS THE FINISH LINE?

Rick and Barbara Cohen (Case Study 5) have been praying for some time about their Eternity Portfolio. In recent years their assets have increased significantly, especially the stock options in Rick's company. Barbara is the founding partner of a small CPA (certified public accounting) firm in San Francisco, where they live, and her business has prospered as well. By all reasonable calculations, Rick and Barbara have more than they will need to support their family going forward.

After much deliberation, the Cohens have decided to exercise and sell a large portion of Rick's stock options and invest $1.7 million in their Eternity Portfolio. They will place part of that amount in a Donor-Advised Fund to be distributed over the coming years, primarily to strategic ministries to the homeless in San Francisco. They intend to invest $2 million in a Charitable Remainder Trust. (We'll talk more about these techniques in chapter 8.) Finally, Rick and Barbara will make additional investments in the years ahead when more of Rick's stock options are exercised and Barbara's CPA firm is sold at retirement.

Note that many people have reached financial independence without a large amount of assets. Case Study 4 gives the example of Ben Richards, who makes $28,000 per year. Ben is a fifty-seven-year-old widower whose children are almost grown. As he looks toward retirement, Ben expects his pension and Social Security benefits to exceed his living expenses. Having accumulated some modest investment assets, Ben decides that he can begin to invest excess cash exclusively in his Eternity Portfolio.

One last example of "How much is enough for good?" is the Fleming family (Case Study 3). Todd and Emily Fleming are in their early forties and have four children, ages eight to fourteen. Todd recently sold his first company, Industrial Solutions, for $30 million. Although he has been told by some well-meaning friends that he should consider retiring to work in some sort of full-time Christian ministry, Todd feels that God really wants him to start a new business. He and Emily believe God has specially equipped Todd to be an entrepreneur. They plan to invest $23 million of the sale proceeds in a new business venture. Next, the Flemings plan to donate $3 million to several strategic ministries, including their church. Finally, the Fleming Family Foundation will be established and funded with $2 million to be used for making later gifts. Emily is also considering the idea of establishing a crisis-pregnancy clinic with funds from the foundation. (We'll discuss more on foundations in chapter 8.)

ADDITIONAL OBSERVATIONS

You may be saying to yourself, "That's great for people who have a lot of money or a nice pension, but what about me? I've been saving for retirement for years but will never have 'enough' based on these definitions." First, take heart; most people are in your same situation and many are worse off. The important thing is to continue to invest in your Eternity Portfolio even while you have the financial independence finish line in front of you.

> For me, dependence is a good thing. Financial dependence puts me in a position of spiritual dependence. The more dependent on God I am, the better off I am!
>
> *Todd Harper*

> It's so easy to think of what I would do with someone else's wealth. Anytime I look at someone with more, God convicts me to think about what I'm doing with what I already have.
>
> *Dr. Johnny Hunt*

It is true that for most people, financial independence will not happen by age fifty-five—and maybe not by sixty-five, either. Is that a bad thing? God created us for work, *even if we don't need the money!* Since many jobs no longer require the physical exertion they once did, we are blessed to live in a period where we can continue to be productive well past the historical retirement age.

I know of a number of people who retired from their jobs and then "retired" from this life shortly thereafter. Their purpose for living was inextricably connected to their employment, but they also wanted to retire at the earliest possible moment. If at all possible, try to find a job you enjoy doing or something that has its own non-financial motivation. That may sound like common sense, but here's the twist: *doing something you actually like might be a reason to take a job where you earn less.* You won't dread every Monday morning, and you won't count down the days till you can punch out at age sixty-five. Use 70 percent as a guideline: Choose a job at which you like at least 70 percent of the activities because every job has aspects we dislike.

Remember, your identity is not ultimately wrapped up in your occupation or how much money you make but in the fact that you are a child of God. Financial independence, like so many things in life, is both a benefit and a burden—a privilege and a responsibility that forces you to ask hard questions about God's calling on your life (Hint: probably not just traveling or playing golf or mah jong. Not that there's anything wrong with those).

This point is key: Your investment in the Eternity Portfolio should not be put on hold until you reach the finish line of financial independence. Chapter 4 discussed making this most-critical investment while at the same time allocating resources to other shorter-term goals, such as retirement. *Financial independence may be merely the opportunity to put your eternal investments into high gear.* It is the chance to finish strong and make extraordinary investments in the latter part of your life. But don't wait. Remember the story of the rich fool in the Bible. He thought he could continue saving for himself, but he didn't realize he had no control over his future (see Luke 12:15–21).

Make sure you are making eternal investments throughout the journey of life so that whenever it does end, you will have made the most of your opportunities.

GENEROSITY AS A WAY OF LIFE: David McKinnon

Financial finish lines, even when achieved, are just another step in the generosity process. As God develops us in response to grace, we become increasingly generous with our time, relationships, social capital, and more.

From our very first meeting over a decade ago, I sensed in David McKinnon a mutual passion for generosity in all its forms. I thought to myself on the flight home from our meeting, "I'd be willing to pay money to spend time with this guy." David and Karen actually hired me to be their family advisor, and we have since become partners in my latest business venture.

Born into a missionary family, David spent his early childhood on the island of Tortola in the British Virgin Islands. As an adult, his ability to connect with people across race, culture, and economic status can probably be traced to that childhood where all his friends had a different skin color. David is a talented entrepreneur with quite a number of business successes over the years. He was recently inducted into the Entrepreneurship Hall of Fame and has received the International Franchise Association's prestigious Entrepreneur of the Year Award, among other honors. No doubt, he is a talented, experienced, CEO-type leader who can build organizations. But I believe the "secret sauce" for David is a generosity of spirit that drives him to give of himself, his social capital, and his possessions in a uniquely

Continued on next page

inspiring way. And he does it almost effortlessly. At one of our first meetings, we were standing in line at a Starbucks when the lady in front of David realized she'd left her purse in the car. Without a second thought, David said, "Put that on my tab." That's just part of a long pattern of generosity I've seen in both David and Karen. In our years of history together, David has never allowed me to pay for a meal. That might not sound remarkable, but I'm pretty quick on the draw for the check myself, and it has been a humbling and valuable lesson for me to experience receiving generosity.

In business and personal relationships, David overflows with generosity that draws people like a magnet. I've marveled at situations in which friends have treated him poorly (even stolen from him) and that generous spirit stays constant and brings reconciliation. He genuinely loves people in a way that appears to be vulnerability—whether in strategic business negotiations or personal conflict resolution. But the providence of God's incredible power overwhelms apparent weakness. David's openness and intentional vulnerability work out deals that make me scratch my head in wonder.

David tells a story about his dad that makes me wonder if generosity is inherited in the DNA, and he's given permission for me to share this personal testimony of God's grace. David remembers a day when he was a boy in Tortola and his father called a family meeting to make a shocking confession. He had fathered a child with the nanny, and they would have to leave their ministry on the island in disgrace. After making the confession, he asked his wife for forgiveness, and then sternly declared they were never to speak of the matter again. The family settled down in Canada, and David grew into a man, but the circumstances on Tortola were never mentioned until, decades later, David's father lay on his deathbed. He whispered to David, "You have a younger brother, Timothy, and I want you to find him once I'm gone." David's mother had already passed away, and David wasn't sure how to even begin tracking down his brother, but the search was on. Eventually he was able to locate his former nanny, Comelia, who was living in Brooklyn, and then Timothy, his half-brother. A remarkable reconciliation began with a Christmas dinner in New York with both families. David always says of that time, "What Christmas present does God give a fifty-year-old white guy who has everything? A six-foot-four African American baby brother!"

But that's not the best part. At dinner, Comelia shared what happened from that fateful day all those years before down in Tortola after the confession. She told David how his mother went immediately to Comelia's house, forgave her for the affair, and cooked a meal for her. Then, for the next twenty years—until Timothy turned twenty-one—David's mother sent money every month to support Comelia and Timothy—all without David's father ever knowing about it. Her legacy of generosity would eventually lead to a loving reconciliation. No wonder David and Karen continue the legacy through their family, friends, business, and ministry. And the kingdom of God advances.

DISCUSSION QUESTIONS

1. What does retirement mean to you? Financial independence? Recreation and relaxation? Moving from full-time to part-time work? An opportunity for ministry?

2. Have you established a financial finish line for your life savings? If so, how has that impacted your outlook on life? On work? On money?

3. Is financial independence a worthy goal for a Christian? Why or why not?

4. Should your life be different once you reach financial independence? If so, how?

5. If you have already reached the point where financially it appears that you have "enough," what are you doing with the excess? Might God be leading you to invest significantly more in your Eternity Portfolio right now?

6. If retirement and financial independence seem out of reach for you, what should your response be?

God's Asset Allocation

6

- God's plan for your giving investments
- Where to invest
- What types of investments to make
- Designing your Eternity Portfolio with focus on your personal mission

Once you really get motivated to start investing, say for retirement, where do you start? Did you know there are literally hundreds of thousands of investments available in the market? Which types will best meet your needs?

Investing strategy begins with funding and then progresses to portfolio design. Although there is certainly room for spontaneous investments, the foundation for a successful portfolio is laid with a well-designed strategy.

In my previous work as a wealth manager, when a new client came to my office, we started with extensive planning. We would spend several hours talking about the broad landscape of investments before I gave specific recommendations. For example, we'd talk about asset allocation, which is the process of deciding which of the major categories of investments such as cash, bonds, stocks, real estate, and commodities (gold, for example)—should be included in the portfolio and to what extent. Only after the portfolio is designed and the different investment categories are identified can the actual investments be made.

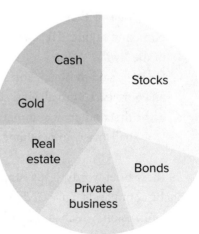

In order to make informed decisions, you must have some understanding of the context of your investments. Studies have shown the effectiveness of an investment portfolio over time is largely determined by design. Having an accurate perspective on the overall investing universe is just as important as selecting the actual investments.

This principle applies to the Eternity Portfolio as well. This chapter is meant to give you the "lay of the land" when it comes to the major design considerations for your Eternity Portfolio. The decision of *how much* to invest is only the first step. Andrew Carnegie summed it up best when he described the difficulty of giving away wealth in a strategic manner: "It is well to remember that it requires the exercise of not less ability than that which acquires it, to use wealth so as to be really beneficial to the community."[1]

As you focus on giving as investing, you quickly realize that the questions of *where, what,* and *how* are the most difficult ongoing decisions for the faithful manager. Fortunately we are not left to figure these out for ourselves. God has clearly described His priorities (or asset classes) for our giving. To be most effective, our eternal investments should align with His overarching purpose. It's not coincidence that these are the same priorities He has for the other parts of our lives.

Let's start with the big picture, which can't get any bigger than the greatest commandments mentioned by Jesus:

> Then one of them, a lawyer, asked Him a question, testing Him, and saying, "Teacher, which is the great commandment in the law?"
>
> Jesus said to him, "'You shall love the Lord your God with all your heart, with all your soul, and with all your mind.' This is the first and great commandment. And the second is like it: 'You shall love your neighbor as yourself.'" (Matthew 22:35–39)

In these brief words, Jesus summarized thousands of years of laws and prophetic commands. *Love God first; then love people.* Jesus also gave us the great commission, which gets a little more specific:

> Go therefore and make disciples of all the nations, baptizing

them in the name of the Father and of the Son and of the Holy Spirit, teaching them to observe all things that I have commanded you; and lo, I am with you always, even to the end of the age. (Matthew 28:19–20)

It's clear that these commands of Jesus should affect the way we live. But they should also affect the way we give! As Christians, we should build our Eternity Portfolio to carry out the great commandments and fund the great commission. The resources God has provided over and above our needs should be invested to share the love of Christ with others.

This chapter will help you understand the investing universe from God's perspective. It is only as you understand the big picture Christian mission that you can identify your part within it and design your Eternity Portfolio accordingly.

We will go through a process that should enable you to build your portfolio design in some detail. Your portfolio will be as individual as everything else about you. If you are married, you and your spouse both need to give input, and you should reach a mutually agreeable solution. For families with children, the Eternity Portfolio is a great starting place to widen their vision for God's kingdom. Each family member can have a part.

As you begin to design your portfolio, ask the following questions:

1. Where should I be making an impact with my giving?
2. What am I trying to accomplish with my giving?
3. How has God specifically gifted and called me to achieve these goals?

INVESTING AS A FAMILY TEAM

(Special thanks to Sharon Epps, co-founder of Women Doing Well, for her insights on this section.)

Most married couples, though they confer about the big issues and decisions, delegate the care of the family finances to one partner or the other—usually to the one who is more interested or better at managing the business details. This natural tendency will probably also apply as

Continued on next page

married couples begin to develop an Eternity Portfolio. But if you are married, be sure your spouse participates in the decision making and giving vision. If ever there was a venture that called for the wisdom of "Two are better than one" (Ecclesiastes 4:9), it's your Eternity Portfolio.

> "Many couples default into either making separate decisions or one spouse makes all of the decisions and assumes that the other spouse would think the same way. Financial planners frequently express frustration in efforts to bring both the husband and wife into the money discussion. . . . Mutual decision-making strengthens the marriage and more accurately reflects the image of God." *Sharon Epps*

If one of you is holding back, consider why that might be. During much of the last century, financial investment was often considered an arena only for men. What a blessing that the wisdom and insight of women are a growing part of the world of investment and giving. Recent research conducted by the organization Women Doing Well shows that the overall giving of a family increases significantly when a woman gets involved in the giving.[3] A global survey showed that when women were asked what was most important to them, they commonly responded, "to help make someone's life better or help make the world a better place."[4] Your family's giving plan needs the compassionate insight of both partners.

Giving strategist and Women Doing Well co-founder Sharon Epps puts her finger on other reasons we might hold back from getting involved in the Eternity Portfolio. One is that we may not have fully embraced God's love. Sharon notes that those who supported Jesus "out of their own means" were those who had fully received Christ's love and healing.[5] When we realize we've received much, it leads to further giving.

Based on the research, another reason women might hold back is a dislike for the world of numbers. "Giving decisions can feel sterile if we don't see the stories behind the numbers," suggests Sharon. "We see giving as unappealing math rather than stories of real people." It helps to "purposefully engage with others' needs," getting to know the real people and the real stories behind the giving opportunity.[6]

Most of all, though, Sharon believes women in particular hold back from getting involved in kingdom investing because they don't realize that God has given them significant influence in the world.[7] Regardless of whether women sport impressive resumes or significant balance sheets, when they're asked, "What do you have?" they frequently understate their influence, resources, and potential impact. Taking the time to list the resources God has given them often helps women embrace the significance of what they manage.

Great conversations between you and your spouse will occur when you ask good questions.

> "Ask great questions to discover your spouse's story and viewpoint: 'What's your greatest wish for the family?' Discover money views: 'What connotation did money hold for you growing up?' Discover where your spouse wants to be headed: 'What are you passionate about?' and 'As you look at the next season of life, where would you like your focus to be?'" *Sharon Epps*

As you grow together in this venture of investing in the kingdom, encourage each other to be transparent with your motivations and desires. Share your values, listening to each other and learning to care about what your spouse cares about.

WHERE?

JERUSALEM, JUDEA, AND THE WORLD

God's plan has always been for the whole world. "For God so loved the *world* that He gave His only begotten Son, that whoever believes in Him should not perish but have everlasting life" (John 3:16, emphasis added). Over the last two thousand years, the good news of Jesus Christ has radiated outward from a small area in the Middle East to most of the known world. This was no accident. Before His ascension to heaven, Jesus left the disciples further instructions about the great commission. He knew that without specific guidance, they might feel their sole responsibility was the nation of Israel. Jesus made it clear that His plan was much bigger than that:

> But you shall receive power when the Holy Spirit has come upon you; and you shall be witnesses to Me in Jerusalem, and in all Judea and Samaria, and to the end of the earth. (Acts 1:8)

The disciples were to impact their local area (Jerusalem), their region (Judea and Samaria), and the whole globe ("the end of the earth"). Jesus entrusts us with the same mission today. God is working around the world, and we want to be a part of it. Therefore, the first level of decision about our Eternity Portfolio is where we will focus our investments.

Scripture mentions a fourth locale in addition to Jerusalem, Judea, and the other parts of the world: Samaria. The Samaritans were part Jewish and part gentile. There was hatred between the Jews and Samaritans. We are encouraged to love, give, and pray for our enemies. God's strategy extends to those who appear to be unlovable and those we are in conflict with. Our Eternity Portfolio is not complete if it does not extend grace and resources to our enemies.

Jack Alexander

Note that many charitable organizations are making a significant impact in more than one area of the world. Churches are a prime example. My church has a major emphasis in all three areas and is making a difference on these fronts simultaneously. Examples include our benevolence ministry to the poor (local), leadership training conferences (regional), and strategic church-planting efforts (global). It can be helpful to attempt to categorize your investments based on their geographic impact.

Local. Most people invest the largest part of their giving locally. Programs that benefit local churches, schools, hospitals, and so forth are popular for obvious reasons: People see the benefit of their giving on a regular basis. Results are easier to measure. Loyalty and a sense of community are also major factors.

We are defining *local* as local to the donor. An example of a local investment is a community homeless shelter. Although the indirect benefits of the organization can certainly reach other areas, the primary focus is meeting the needs of the local population.

You will probably want to have a significant part of your portfolio focused locally because of the witness this represents in the community. "The light that shines farthest shines brightest at home." Our platform for personal witness often begins with investments close to home.

Regional. Regional investments extend our view beyond community to the outer reaches of our cultural boundaries. An organization ministering across the United States would be an example. Also included in this category would be a ministry focused on a particular area, need, or people group (e.g., Native Americans) here in the United States.

The advantage of the regional category is obviously that it directly impacts more people than a local ministry. In the normal growth process of a successful ministry, there is a natural tendency to expand coverage area. This can bring a whole set of new challenges as the organization grows, however, and must be done with care.

Global. Global investments are focused outside our cultural boundaries. They might also work within our region or local area, but the main thrust is elsewhere around the world. An example might be a relief organization that works all over the world to reduce poverty and hunger.

Compared to local or even regional investments, there are significant advantages and disadvantages, from the investor's perspective, to global organizations. One major advantage is the lower cost of living in many countries as compared to the United States. Money just goes farther. Another advantage is that the "harvest" can be much higher if God is really moving in one country versus another. For example, in the last twenty years, Christianity has swept across countries in Africa and even China while experiencing a decline or very little growth in Europe. The major disadvantage is that the long-distance nature of the projects makes accountability much more difficult.

> Here's an idea: take a few minutes to look at your giving from the past year or two and separate the donations out into the three geographical buckets. Does there need to be further differentiation to make it more clear (i.e., parsing out "local" into your city and county separately, or parsing out "global" into Africa and Latin America)?
>
> Once you've done this, estimate the percentage of your giving that falls into each geographical category and then ask yourself whether that mix makes your heart sing. If it doesn't, ask God to reveal the right geographical mix for your giving and switch things up to a mix of local/regional/global that you have joy about and feel led to by the Lord.
>
> *Heather Tuininga*

WHAT?

REACHING, TEACHING, AND MINISTERING TO NEEDS

Jesus instructed us to go into all the world and make disciples. Along the way we are to share Christ's love by loving our neighbors as ourselves. This missional focus can be broken out into three broad tasks:

1. Gospel: Reaching people with the good news of Christ
2. Discipleship: Teaching Christians biblical truth about how to live as followers of Christ

3. Mercy and justice: Ministering to people's physical, emotional, and spiritual needs in the name of Christ

These three categories are straight out of the great commandments and great commission. All of the investments we make in the Eternity Portfolio fall into these three broad "asset classes." Let's look at each class in more detail.

GOD'S ASSET ALLOCATION

GOSPEL: SPREADING THE GOOD NEWS OF THE KINGDOM

Throughout history faithful men and women have funded God's prophets, evangelists, and preachers. From Elijah (1 Kings 17) to the disciples (Luke 9), God has used His people to invest in the spread of the gospel. Jesus spoke about the importance of supporting this effort:

> He who receives you receives Me, and he who receives Me receives Him who sent Me. He who receives a prophet in the name of a prophet shall receive a prophet's reward. And he who receives a righteous man in the name of a righteous man shall receive a righteous man's reward. And whoever gives one of these little ones only a cup of cold water in the name of a disciple, assuredly, I say to you, he shall by no means lose his reward. (Matthew 10:40–42)

You can be involved in funding the gospel in many different ways. These range from the obvious—such as giving to a citywide outreach event—to the not-so-obvious—such as investing in a ministry that translates Scripture into different languages.

Many organizations within the Christian community have evangelistic motives. However, when building your portfolio, keep in mind we are looking at the *focus* of the ministry as a differentiator.

The major sectors within gospel organizations include Bible translation/distribution, church planting, and group/event focus. There can be additional categories within each of these.

Bible translation/distribution is a straightforward category describing those organizations committed to making the Word of God available to people in all languages around the world.

Church planting includes organizations as well as individuals who develop strategies and train pastors to start Christian communities in traditional and nontraditional settings. In some countries these churches are simply groups of believers meeting in each other's homes. Many missionaries are part of the church-planting category.

Finally, **group/event** focus tends to be the "large numbers" strategies such as crusades, festivals, and other gatherings intended to expose many people at a time to the message of Jesus Christ. Also within this category are organizations that use a specific activity as an opportunity to reach out within the community while offering an important service. Sports camps and school campus programs would be examples of this type of organization.

GOSPEL

Church planting	Bible translation and distribution	Group/Event focus

Explore the different opportunities and learn where God is working. You may be surprised at the sheer magnitude of what is going on in every facet of life. For example, in the athletics arena, a program called Upward Basketball began as a way to help local children through organized sports. An athletic league that is open to the public, Upward Basketball holds practices and games at the church sponsoring the program. At each event there is a break in the activity, and one of the participants shares a testimony about what God has done in his or her life. As this program has spread through churches around the country, it has expanded to include cheerleading, soccer, and other sports. Investing in Upward Basketball is a way to share the good news of Jesus Christ.

On a completely different front, some of the most strategic activity in the world today is happening through partnerships with groups of believers in different countries. For example, local leaders in India are empowered and resourced by partners in the United States. Cultural differences can be appreciated and the message contextualized by Christians who are natural leaders in their own countries. In this way, church planting *movements* have experienced exponential (as opposed to additive) growth across whole regions.

It would be hard to overestimate the impact of Christians investing selflessly in this area. Listen to the following account:

> The history of the first two centuries of Christianity abounds with remarkable facts, showing with what zeal and entireness of soul, the church went into the work of converting the world. Those who periled their lives and suffered the loss of all things in preaching, were not the only ones who made sacrifices for the spread of the gospel. Some spent all besides a bare support of themselves, to furnish the means of evangelizing others; those who had no property gave the avails of their labor; and it is recorded of one man that he sold himself as a slave to a heathen family, to get access to them for their conversion, and for years cheerfully endured the labor and condition of a slave till he succeeded with the whole family, and took his liberty from the gratitude of the converts. . . . The fires of such benevolence, burning wherever a company of Christians was gathered, could not fail soon to overspread the world, and in the space of one generation most of the nations then known to the civilized world, were more or less evangelized. And if such a tone of benevolent action could be now restored to the church, another generation would not pass before the earth would be 'full of the knowledge and glory of God, as the waters cover the sea.[8]

DISCIPLESHIP

The second major asset class within the Eternity Portfolio is discipleship—the opportunity to invest in people and organizations focused on the spiritual growth of the church. The apostle Paul spent much of his time teaching new converts how to be fully devoted followers of Jesus Christ. Paul generated much of his own support through his secular trade of tent making, but he gave clear, common-sense guidance in this area: "Let him who is taught the word share in all good things with him who teaches" (Galatians 6:6). Elsewhere, when speaking of teachers, Jesus stated that "the laborer is worthy of his wages" (Luke 10:7).

Within the Christian community today, there are many different types of organizations aimed at discipleship. The major categories include counseling, Christian education, and research or curriculum development.

Counseling ministries focus on the one-on-one interaction that can take place over a variety of topics including marriage, finances, and spiritual growth. The purpose is to help Christians (and often non-Christians) overcome obstacles in their lives and serve God more fully.

Christian education is typically broad-based group discipleship. Radio programs, Bible studies, Christian schools and universities—all these and more fall into this category.

> There is a stronger need for [giving to educational programs] today than ever in our history. As our institutions of learning are becoming more secular, even more atheistic. I have heard it said that over 70% of kids from Christian homes who go off to secular universities leave their faith while there.
>
> *Lorne Jackson*

The last category, **research and curriculum development**, is composed of organizations primarily focused on developing and producing discipleship tools (such as apologetics or small-group studies). Other organizations address political, scientific, or medical issues from a Christian worldview.

DISCIPLESHIP

Counseling	Christian education	Research/curriculum development

MERCY AND JUSTICE

Ministering to the needs of the poor receives more explicit emphasis in the Bible than any other area of giving. Verse after verse encourages those who love God to engage in this tangible expression of His love for others. Let's look at just a few of the many verses:

> If there is among you a poor man of your brethren, within any of the gates in your land which the Lord your God is giving you, you shall not harden your heart nor shut your hand from your poor brother. (Deuteronomy 15:7)

> Blessed is he who considers the poor; the Lord will deliver him in time of trouble. The Lord will preserve him and keep him alive, and he will be blessed on the earth. (Psalm 41:1–2)

> He who has pity on the poor lends to the Lord, and He will pay back what he has given. (Proverbs 19:17)

> He who has a generous eye will be blessed, for he gives of his bread to the poor. (Proverbs 22:9)

It was obvious from His teaching and actions that Jesus was passionate about the plight of the poor, the sick, and the helpless. He fed them, healed them, and gave them hope regularly during His earthly ministry. When He counseled the rich young ruler, Jesus indicated that giving to the poor would result in treasure in heaven for those who followed Him:

> Jesus said to him, "If you want to be perfect, go, sell what you have and give to the poor, and you will have treasure in heaven; and come, follow Me." (Matthew 19:21)

As the love of Christ is lived out in our lives, a natural result is that we love helping people, especially those who can't help themselves. We can also see this emphasis in the early church, which organized a task force for collecting and administering gifts to the poor (see Acts 4:32–37; 6:1–7). And Paul was continuously taking up money for the poor as he traveled from church to church (see Romans 15:25–27; 2 Corinthians 8–9).

The mercy and justice category can be divided into four main areas. The first resides at the most basic level of human need: **food/clothing/shelter.** In addition to obvious investments such as homeless shelters and food pantries, this includes humanitarian relief organizations in war-torn and poverty-stricken regions around the world.

Another subcategory is **health care**, which covers research, treatment, and preventive measures. Free or discounted health clinics, humanitarian medical care in foreign countries, hospice care centers—all are examples of this category.

And then there is **life-skills training**, which focuses on training, literacy, and microenterprise as a means to break the poverty cycle. For example, there are organizations and some churches that provide training such as ESL (English as a second language) and computer skills. Microenterprise is a relatively new concept in the international community whereby people or groups make small loans—maybe just $100—to individuals who use the funds to start a business making textiles, farming, and so on.

MERCY & JUSTICE

Food/Shelter/ Clothing	Healthcare	Legal & Political Systems	Life skills training

Justice is an important but often overlooked aspect of helping the disadvantaged. Even in the West, but particularly in developing nations, **legal and political systems** often work against the poor and powerless, and authorities do not enforce laws to protect human rights. Christians must work to address systematic injustice through legal and political channels, working to change the system. We can provide advocates for those who are unable to represent themselves, whether due to poverty, lack of education, or social stigma. In Luke 11:42, Jesus criticized the Pharisees for ignoring justice. And in Matthew 25 He spoke of compassion for the "least of these," from the stranger to the prisoner. Mercy and justice are deeply connected. Christ has loved us and given Himself for us, and we pattern our behavior after His. Although often with the same constituency, justice is more about addressing systems that favor the powerful over the weak. Those working to create real change in this space must be in it for the long haul. Human social systems don't change quickly and power structures tend to reinforce themselves.

> Justice involves using our social (connections and relationships) and financial capital to bring about fairness and blessing to the poor and minorities. There are both personal and systemic injustices. A friend recently asked how I use my "majority status" to influence the lives of those less fortunate. For years, we have been supporting more than 1000 widows in India whose farmer husbands all committed suicide. We have also supported International Justice Mission, which works to eliminate slavery and trafficking in India and other places. This is an example of addressing issues of both justice and mercy.
>
> *Jack Alexander*

> I love the concept of microenterprise giving and have been involved with a large charity in Canada that does this well. My wife and I have traveled to some countries to see microenterprise at work. This charity not only helps the poor provide for themselves, but they do it with dignity and also teach on evangelism and discipleship. They do all of this with the local people providing the service.
>
> *Lorne Jackson*

There are two main reasons to invest in mercy and justice. First, helping those who cannot help themselves is an outward display of the love of God in your heart. John wrote of this to the early Christians:

> By this we know love, because He laid down His life for us. And we also ought to lay down our lives for the brethren. But whoever has this world's goods, and sees his brother in need, and shuts up his heart from him, how does the love of God abide in him? (1 John 3:16–17)

James, the brother of Jesus, carries this theme in his writing as well:

> Pure and undefiled religion before God and the Father is this:
> to visit orphans and widows in their trouble. (James 1:27)

Caring for the poor has been a hallmark of Christian love from the very beginning. Reports such as the following were common:

> And their kindness to the poor was boundless. Christians felt as much bound to this as to prayer, or to the hearing of the gospel. Contributions and actual exertions for their relief were made indispensable parts of Sabbath exercises. At the close of public worship, lists of the needy, the widows and orphans, were produced and considered, and additions were made from time to time as new cases occurred; and the wants of these were supplied from the funds gathered by free contributions. No heart-stirring appeals were needed to awake dormant sympathies.[9]

The second big reason you want to invest in the mercy and justice sector is that, in many ways, it is the *facilitator* of the other parts of the Christian mission. Critical physical needs are felt more strongly than spiritual needs. If a person is starving, he likely won't be able to consider spiritual issues until his hunger is satisfied.

My former business partner Dave Polstra coordinates a medical partnership between several U.S. churches and a church in Guatemala. Teams of doctors, dentists, and assistants from the United States make trips to Guatemala to provide medical services to people in mountain villages. As part of their visit to the clinic, the local people have the opportunity to hear about Jesus and understand the love that compels these volunteers to share of their time, skills, and money.

BLENDED INVESTMENTS

What about an organization that teaches soil conservation and microfarming in Zimbabwe, or a group that runs a "test prep" academy in Rwanda to facilitate students being accepted to universities in the United States?

Where would these fit in the portfolio? Both organizations use the Bible as a key teaching tool and share the gospel as a core element. Are they gospel or discipleship ministries? I would actually classify them as mercy and justice because the main purpose of both organizations is helping poor and disadvantaged people. Many organizations focus on more than one major area. From a practical *and* theological sense, it is often difficult to tell where mercy ends and gospel begins, or where gospel ends and discipleship begins. That's perfectly okay. In fact, many organizations will have elements of each. There is crossover in the subcategories as well: the Rwandan academy is about education for the students but also encourages the students, once educated, to return and become strong leaders in Rwanda, acting as a force for good in the political and legal system. There is no need to make rigid distinctions when building your portfolio. However, when evaluating investments, I have found it helpful to identify the *major thrust* of an organization, which helps me compare and decide whether it fits my specific calling as an investor.

> This is another chance for you to look at your past or current giving to see how it fits into these categories of gospel, discipleship, mercy, and justice. Are there things that don't fit at all? Estimate the percentage of your giving in each category and ask God if that is how He wants you investing the funds in your Eternity Portfolio.
>
> *Heather Tuininga*

HOW?

YOUR UNIQUE OPPORTUNITIES

Hugh O. Maclellan Jr. heads up the Maclellan Foundation, a large Christian grant-making foundation in Chattanooga, Tennessee. As one in a long line of faithful managers, he has spent years refining the giving strategy of his own family as well as that of the Maclellan Foundation. Hugh talks about the way he and his wife have built their Eternity Portfolio, which starts at 70 percent of their income. First, they allocate 10 percent of their income to their local church. Then 15 percent goes to what they call "small sustaining" gifts. These include helping needy families as the opportunities arise, "dollar swapping" (you support my favorite charity, I'll support yours), and other gifts of encouragement that arise spontaneously. The final and largest area of the Maclellan's personal giving is 45 percent to what they consider strategic investments. Their two major focuses in their strategic category are evangelism and mercy.

By now you have gotten a sense for the Eternity Portfolio investing universe, and we can now look at how those fit into your particular portfolio. Even though you may not be investing 70 percent of your income, you can still be just as strategic with how you allocate your giving. It takes time and intentional focus, but as you design your portfolio, there are some parameters you will want to consider. Start with a framework something like this:

DESIGNING MY ETERNITY PORTFOLIO

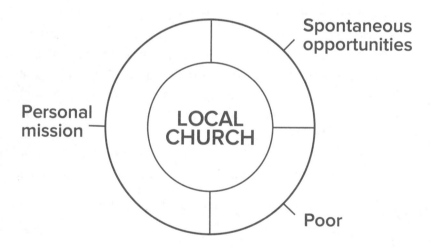

THE LOCAL CHURCH—A CORE INVESTMENT

When designing the stock portion of a traditional investment portfolio, the first thing we install is a core holding of large U.S. company stocks. The purpose of this core holding is to provide solid long-term returns in an area of the market (large multinational corporations) that has been well defined and evaluated over many decades. For some people with limited resources, this may be their entire portfolio strategy. Those who have larger portfolios take advantage of other more focused investments (those with higher risk/return potential) in addition to the core holding.

In much the same way, you can view systematic giving to your local church as a core investment in your Eternity Portfolio. Strategic, discipling churches that are committed to the Holy Scriptures and fulfilling the great commission make a powerful difference for the kingdom of God. Let me share six key reasons why your Eternity Portfolio should start with at least a 10 percent investment in your church.

1. **Informed, coordinated effort.** The church is uniquely positioned to be aware of needs in the local community and to guide the activity of its members to effective ministry. The book of Acts describes how early church members brought their gifts to the leaders, who organized and directed their use (see Acts 4, 6).

2. **Diversification.** Strategic churches have paid staff and volunteers who, working as a team, are able to focus simultaneously on specific elements of the threefold mission: gospel, discipleship, and mercy and justice. Nowhere else will you find this immediate coverage of all "asset classes" in your portfolio.

3. **Worship.** Giving is supremely an act of worship. Just as you regularly focus on prayer, praise, and preaching during church services, the giving process is a vital part of worship.

4. **Personal benefit.** I am frequently amazed at the way many Christians enjoy the benefits of church programs, facilities, and support without ever feeling compelled to help fund them. Invest in the organizations that are contributing to the spiritual, social, and physical development of you and your family.

5. **Personal opportunity.** The church presents your best opportunity to be involved *with* your investment. In addition to your money, you can invest freely of your time and abilities. Your church offers on-the-job training and involvement in almost every sphere of ministry.

6. **Accountability.** Few organizations have as much transparency to the donor as the local church. Typically within the church you have welcome access to the senior pastor, key department directors, and the annual budget. You are able to see firsthand the results of your investment.

> The local church is the hub of my giving. Christ has made the greatest investment in my life, however, the church follows behind Christ in that only Heaven knows where I would be without His body's investment and challenge in my life.
>
> *Dr. Johnny Hunt*

PERSONAL MISSION: FOCUS ON YOUR CALLING

The mission of the church is quite broad. However, God has equipped each member to be most effective in his or her area of special calling.

> Now you are the body of Christ, and members individually. And God has appointed these in the church: first apostles, second prophets, third teachers, after that miracles, then gifts of healings, helps, administrations, varieties of tongues. Are all apostles? Are all prophets? Are all teachers? (1 Corinthians 12:27–29)

In this passage Paul is saying we are each uniquely gifted and motivated. Determine where your calling lies and pursue it with your time, abilities, and investments. For example, one of Hugh Maclellan's passions is evangelism, and in particular church planting. He invests the strategic section of his Eternity Portfolio in his calling. In my case, my strategic investments are in discipleship and poverty relief (specifically in the areas of faithful life management, leadership training, and entrepreneurship). Not only do I focus my money there, I also spend much of my time in those activities.

> How is God working in your life to show you what you love? The further you go with God, seeking Him, the more your heart is drawn to the things He wants. And He shows us through both pain and passion—they are like first cousins.
>
> *Jack Alexander*

Focus a significant portion of your "nonchurch" investing on your God-given calling in ministry. It is also quite possible that some of your most strategic opportunities will arise within your local church. From a portfolio management standpoint, I would classify those investments under your personal mission.

Perhaps you have no idea of the personal mission to which God has called you. That's okay, but start searching now. Begin praying for God to specifically lead you to His plan. Study the Bible for insight. You may find yourself drawn to a broad area, such as gospel, and then gradually realize your gifts fit with something more specific within that area, such as counseling at a citywide outreach festival. Or your calling may come the other way around: first you sense God laying on your heart a passion for helping women in crisis pregnancies, and later you begin to understand how that fits in the broader area of mercy and justice. Seek God's will in prayer and Bible study.

As God leads, invest your money. The intersection of your personal mission with your giving is one of the most powerful combinations you can experience. True joy and fulfillment in Christ are the result of aligning your life with God's purpose. Your effectiveness for the kingdom of God will multiply exponentially as you move in this direction.

> When it comes to personal mission, possibly the most significant thing we do with "type A" entrepreneurs is help them redefine what they're solving for. It's a whole new ballgame when we change the variable we are solving for—instead of maximizing net worth, we look to maximize kingdom impact!
>
> *Todd Harper*

REMEMBER THE POOR

Based on the overwhelming coverage of the topic in Scripture, I can only conclude that God *really* wants us to give to the poor. In no other specific area of giving do we see such repeated promises of blessing for obedience and warning for failure. God wants us to take the time and invest resources to help those who cannot help themselves and who will not be able to reciprocate.

I cannot help but think that a major part of God's plan to reveal Himself to the world is through the righteous and selfless acts of Christians. We need to get in on this plan.

Unfortunately, waste and corruption have often been the hallmark of government welfare programs. This is a grave concern to us as strategic investors; we have no interest in funding programs that perpetuate the poverty cycle or giving money that is siphoned to special-interest groups. However, the potential for abuse does not lessen our responsibility to remember the poor. There *are* organizations that operate effectively in this sector. If you take the time to understand the organizations you support, you can reduce the likelihood that your investment will be wasted or mismanaged. (We'll talk more about this concept in chapter 7.) When it comes to gifts to help struggling families or individuals, we should try for discernment but err on the side of generosity. There is no telling how God will use your gifts to make a difference for someone else.

I have found this principle [taking the time to understand] to be true again and again. I once worked with a family who was being asked to fund a new project for a ministry they liked in Uganda. The past projects had gone fine, so they were excited to step into this new idea. The project was to buy some land and have the families in the surrounding villages come together to plant and harvest from the land. I was already headed to Uganda to check out a few other potential investments for their Eternity Portfolio, so I decided to meet up with the guys running this ministry to learn more about the farming project. I had a Ugandan friend with me who was a university-trained agronomist, which ended up being very helpful. They took us out to the land they were proposing to buy and farm. My agronomist friend leaned over to me and said: "Look over there. See that hillside?" I wasn't sure what he was getting at yet. He then had me turn and look the opposite way, and he

> said, "Do you see that hillside? Where do you think the rains go when they come down those hillsides?" The lightbulb went on: this "field" was going to be a floodplain during the rainy season, and any crops the families planted would likely be washed away every six months. The families this project was supposed to help would end up investing tons of sweat equity to plow and plant the field and then get little or no harvest.
>
> *Heather Tuininga*

My wife, Melissa, was recently concerned about a family in our church who were having a difficult time financially. As we discussed how God might want us to be involved in helping, Melissa decided to call some mutual friends to see if they wanted to participate in the joy of what was to be an anonymous "investment pool." The response was overwhelming. In a matter of days, she collected a sizable gift from about ten families. When Melissa passed along the money to the family, she said simply that the funds had been "given to us to give to them." That is how God planned it. He gives us money, some of which is meant for others. The response from this grateful family was praise to God for how He had answered their prayers through an unknown source. They said that in the past God had blessed them to be able to give to others, and now they were on the receiving end.

> In Luke 16:9, Jesus urges us to "use worldly wealth to gain friends for yourselves. Then when your earthly possessions are gone, they will welcome you to an eternal home." Jesus is not suggesting that we "buy friends" but rather teaching that our generosity can appropriately bless others and impact relationships and that these relationships will extend into eternity.
>
> *Jack Alexander*

SPONTANEOUS GIVING: READY FOR THE UNEXPECTED
Spontaneous giving brings joy. Sometimes the opportunity is a missionary in a developing country who needs a new power generator. Maybe a family just lost their home in a flood. It could be a new, radical discipling strategy or a matching-grant opportunity.

Whatever the cause, most of us are wired to respond to urgent cries for help. The problem arises when we must look around for available funds to meet that need—which typically means unplanned personal sacrifice. Now you have a doubly complicated decision: *Should I help with this present situation, and if so, where do I cut back personally to free up the cash?*

My recommendation is that you allocate some funds in your Eternity Portfolio to a category called "spontaneous" or "other" for unanticipated giving opportunities. This concept has made all the difference in the joy Melissa and I feel in giving. Because we have set aside funds specifically for the purpose of investing in new ways, we are actively looking for where God would have us direct that money.

There will also be times you are led to make some truly sacrificial, unplanned investments. Faith is really tested as you decide whether to follow or ignore God's leading. Don't miss the blessing just because it seems to be outside of your systematic strategy. There is an indescribable joy that comes from seeing God work in unusual ways through you. Of course, the wisdom to know whether a particular opportunity is from God comes only after much time spent in communion with Him.

To plan for spontaneous giving, create a special fund for it. I call this my Psalm 23:5 Fund because my cup *does* overflow. A "Generosity Roadmap" (or giving plan) is also something my husband and I put together every year just before the new year begins. We talk through our giving in the past and assess both the impact the funds had and the joy we felt from those donations. Then we pray and talk through the amount we want to give in the coming year (each year God has called us to increase that amount, regardless of what our income is doing; it's challenging, but fun to watch Him show up!), how much we want to go to the church and how much to other organizations that are doing God's work. We write it all down in our Generosity Roadmap and then set aside an amount to go into the Psalm 23:5 Fund for spontaneous giving throughout the year. We get to be intentional in giving to the church and causes God has called us to support, but also available for neat opportunities that come up throughout the year that might not be on our roadmap.

Heather Tuininga

BRINGING IT ALL TOGETHER

This graphic shows the four stages of developing one's Eternity Portfolio: the three eternal asset classes; subsectors of those asset classes; categories of your own unique opportunities and mission; and finally specific investments.

Once you have mapped out your portfolio design, it's time to begin the implementation and choose your specific investments. In the next chapter, we'll look at approaches to wise, strategic decisions for your Eternity Portfolio.

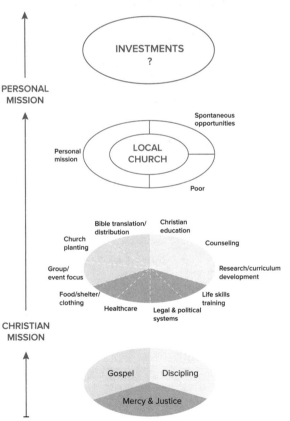

MY ETERNITY PORTFOLIO

DISCUSSION QUESTIONS

1. How might thinking about your giving in terms of a portfolio of investments change your perspective?

2. What do you think about the idea that God has given instructions in the Bible for maximizing your Eternity Portfolio? Do you agree with the three "asset classes" of gospel, discipleship, and mercy and justice? If not, what do you think is missing?

3. In the past, how have you thought about giving to the poor? How has God molded your views in this area? Based on what you read in Scripture, should your current giving have a greater or lesser emphasis on the poor?

4. If you have not supported your local church in the past, why not? Did any of the six reasons on page 147 convince you to begin? If you have faithfully supported your local church, how has that impacted you? What results have you seen?

5. Have you ever thought about your personal mission? After reading the information in this chapter, in what areas do you believe God would have you focus your giving?

6. How can you be more sensitive to God's leading as it relates to spontaneous giving opportunities? Does your Eternity Portfolio currently include a category for this so that money is available when needed?

Making Wise Investments

■ Accountability and your Eternity Portfolio
■ What to look for in a good investment
■ Asking the right questions
■ The Eternity Portfolio investment policy statement

Think about your retirement portfolio for a moment. How did you choose your investments? For example, once you made the decision to invest in stocks, how did you select them? Did you receive a phone call from the CEO of a new company and decide on the spot to invest your hard-earned money in his venture? Maybe you scanned the list of publicly traded stocks in *The Wall Street Journal* and selected a handful of noteworthy companies. Or an acquaintance e-mailed you about a startup company with a great idea for reaching a vast, untapped market. She had just invested some money in the company and thought it would be a great opportunity for you as well.

Any of this sound familiar? The irony is that these scenarios could describe either the typical investing process *or* the giving process of many individuals. Unfortunately, *every year* much of what people believe to be invested for eternity is lost due to ill-conceived strategies, poor management, lack of vision, or just downright ineptitude. And many donors neither realize nor care that this is happening.

STRIVING FOR ACCOUNTABILITY

Although we may receive an annual report from the organizations we support, it can be woefully lacking in the sort of performance data we demand from our traditional investments. Once we make a gift, we often assume our responsibility in the process has ended—or, more likely, we simply forget about it. This is exacerbated by the fact that some charities don't seem motivated to report on how funds have been used until they approach you for the next "investment"—and then only if the results were favorable. (However, some organizations are excellent at keeping donors updated; not surprisingly, these strategic ministries receive more funding and tend to be more effective over the long term.)

Another reason most people "never look back" when it comes to giving is that they themselves do not feel *accountable* for their giving decisions. After all, it's not the same as your retirement portfolio where a poor decision can set back your retirement date a few years. Or is it? Until you develop a true understanding of eternal rewards, your gifts will have no long-term significance to you personally.

Accountability is the key. Whether managing a traditional investment portfolio or the Eternity Portfolio, faithful managers are accountable and *require* this virtue in their investments.

Accountability for the investor involves researching, evaluating, and monitoring investments to achieve the best long-term results for the portfolio. This includes holding organizations accountable for achieving their stated objectives efficiently and on a timely basis. For Christian organizations, we would add "in a way that glorifies God."

Accountability begets results like nothing else on earth. Like most people, I do not like to be accountable to others. However, I have found that I *do like* the results that accountability pushes me to achieve.

> As someone who advises families on their philanthropy, this concept [accountability] makes a ton of sense. If I recommend an investment to the family benefactors that turns out to be a bad choice, I feel bad about that and regret "wasting" their giving funds. It's no different for us if we make bad decisions about investing the ultimate Benefactor's (God's) money.
>
> *Heather Tuininga*

Dr. Bill Bright, founder of Campus Crusade for Christ, gives the following exhortation on strategic giving:

> I encourage you to use the "sound mind" principle to help you determine where to invest in Christ's kingdom. Avoid

emotional giving. Giving on impulse just for the sake of giving or contributing where your gifts are likely to be misused or wasted is not only poor stewardship, but is also contrary to the will of God and grieves the Spirit. Perhaps you have received requests from organizations inviting you to invest in their various projects. Carefully evaluate the worthiness of the ministry you choose and the sincerity of the people involved, and respond to the leading of the Holy Spirit.[1]

> Remember, when it comes to outcomes, we are called to be wise and faithful but not perfect.
>
> *Larry Powell*

This chapter will help you select the actual investments for your Eternity Portfolio. In the search for strategic, long-term investments, we discuss the following key questions:

- How many investments should I make?
- What types of investments should I consider?
- Where will I find them?
- How do I evaluate a specific investment?

Much of what we cover is particularly applicable to gifts you give to a nonprofit organization—not as much to gifts made *directly* to the poor or needy. Although these investments are an important part of your portfolio, their nature does not lend itself so much to strategic evaluation and planning. However, investments in *organizations* whose mission is to reach the poor are included in the coming discussion.

HOW MANY INVESTMENTS SHOULD MY PORTFOLIO CONTAIN?

Sometimes people get caught up in random giving to just about any organization or individual who asks. Large sums of money are dispersed in tiny pieces in somewhat of a "mile wide, inch deep" philosophy. So, for example, it's not unusual for a donor involved in Christian circles to give to dozens of organizations each year out of habit or simply because it's easier to send a small check than to tell someone no. Furthermore, generous people want to give; as they do, the number of people requesting funds naturally multiplies. Even with good intentions, giving can become haphazard. Strategic investments, on the other hand, take money *and* time, both of which are in limited supply.

The most effective giving strategy is one concentrated on a manageable number of focused organizations. Most families could reasonably manage somewhere between one and five additional strategic investments (in addition to direct gifts to the poor and spontaneous onetime gifts), assuming their church is the diversified core of their investment strategy. Institutions such as private foundations with paid staff could conceivably manage a larger number of investments.

You have a limited amount of time to spend managing your Eternity Portfolio. It's probably unrealistic for you to keep abreast of the activities of dozens of different organizations. Another factor is dedicating the most powerful combination of your money and abilities to ministries working in the area of your personal mission. For most people, there is no way to do this with more than two or three major commitments. Finally, from a monetary standpoint, you will have greater impact by making larger gifts to fewer organizations. The ability to fund specific projects or make a substantial difference in a capital campaign comes from these large gifts.

> Givers experiencing the greatest joy in their giving have aligned their life purpose, primary passions, and their kingdom investments.
>
> *Todd Harper*

WHAT TYPES OF INVESTMENTS SHOULD I CONSIDER?

There are no hard-and-fast guidelines for choosing ministries for your Eternity Portfolio. Sometimes God uses organizations that are not considered strategic by anyone's definition. Sometimes. That being said, there are three defining characteristics that tend to mark a project or organization for strategic, long-term success. I use these three marks as my initial screen to determine if I should investigate the organization further.

1. **Inspiring leadership.** It has been said that "everything rises and falls on leadership," and that is certainly true when it comes to investment opportunities. Effective leaders will be passionate, innovative risk-takers who inspire others to follow. They may not be flamboyant or even extroverted, but the fire that burns inside for their mission will likely be evident whether you observe them in person, see them in a video, or read their words in a brochure.

2. **Focused mission.** No ministry can be all things to all people. You want to make an investment in a specific organization for a specific purpose. Make sure it has one. You are right to be skeptical of the one-man startup ministry whose mission statement is "Reaching the whole world with the gospel of Jesus Christ." No matter how admirable the goal, effective ministries start with a specific target opportunity. The vision can certainly expand as God grows the breadth and depth of the organization. But when it comes to strategic investments, look for the laser beam, not the shotgun approach.

3. **Multiplying effect.** What is the "leverage potential" of the investment? Leverage is the ability to make 1+1=3 or 2×3=100. As you evaluate investments, look for opportunities to multiply the effectiveness of your gift. For example, an individual missionary you support may have the potential to reach hundreds of individuals personally with the gospel during a given year. However, a video project on the life of Christ could impact millions of people in one year. This doesn't mean you shouldn't support the individual; however, that investment may be better classified elsewhere in the portfolio. Focus your strategic, personal-mission allocation on exponential growth opportunities.

I have been involved with a ministry that invites pastors from all over the world to participate with their spouses in three days of training and encouragement conducted by veteran pastors and ministry leaders. As is common in small churches, these attendee pastors are overworked and underappreciated, and many are fast approaching burnout. After three days of rest and discipling, they are ready to return home with renewed excitement for their calling. My investment in this pastor discipleship ministry is leveraged across the hundreds of individual congregations representing thousands of individuals these pastors shepherd. The lives that are changed create a multiplying effect.

WHERE DO I FIND INVESTMENT OPPORTUNITIES?

The more engaged you are in the giving process, the more God opens the door to potential investments. Sometimes this is the natural result of heightened awareness.

For us, this started in our local church. We have always supported the church financially and have often made special contributions for specific needs. However, as we became more involved, other ministry opportunities arose. As God began to show us a calling in the area of discipling people in stewardship, we partnered with an organization that provided a small-group study on this subject. Working closely with the local organization's leadership to coordinate the startup in our church, we became aware of the impact this small-group study was having around the country. Melissa and I decided to make an investment in the organization, and our contributions continue to this day. The point is that many times your best giving opportunities come out of the places where you are already serving.

Another important pipeline for investments is your personal relationships. Ask your friends, acquaintances at church, and especially your pastor. Chances are there are many unique ministries operating throughout your spheres of influence. Some time ago, I was looking for an opportunity to be more involved in evangelism outside the United States. Soon I became aware of two strategic opportunities involving church-planting movements—one in India, the other in Europe. God brought these to my attention through personal relationships.

> I have a large *number* of investments in my giving portfolio, however the largest investments are in the ones where my passion mostly lies. I love to give encouraging gifts to ministries that do not necessarily fit my primary callings.
>
> *Dr. Johnny Hunt*

If your church is making a difference in people's lives, it is probably an incubator for new ministries. Not only might you find some great opportunities, you will have the best chance to know the leadership firsthand and be a part of the ministry. However, use caution; startups are very tricky both in business and in ministry. The upside is that you can have a significant impact on some of tomorrow's strategic organizations as an early-stage investor. The downside is that many ministries won't make it, and choosing the "winners" is difficult. You may consider setting aside a certain portion of your portfolio just for startup organizations.

The Internet is growing by leaps and bounds as a source of information on giving investments. Not only can you learn more about an organization, but ratings organizations such as Guidestar and Charity Navigator track financial and operational metrics across a broad spectrum to allow for comparability.

Another resource is your local office of the National Christian Foundation (NationalChristian.com). Chances are the professionals there will be able to help you connect with organizations right in your sweet spot. And, for those who have a Donor-Advised Fund at NCF, your account gives access to a database of ministry profiles. See more on NCF in Appendix D.

The more you pursue God's calling through your personal mission, the more opportunities you will find to invest. Giving will always be a relationship business. As your giving network expands, there will increasingly be more than you can handle. Then comes the challenge of selecting the best investments for your Eternity Portfolio.

HOW DO I EVALUATE A SPECIFIC INVESTMENT?

In the world of investing there is a concept called due diligence. Before an investment manager buys stock in a company, he or she goes through a formal evaluation to determine how well the company compares to other investment opportunities. The manager rigorously examines the company's financial statements, visits the company, and listens as company management presents its strategic plan. The manager keeps asking pertinent questions and documents the results of this inquiry for future reference. Finally, the manager makes the decision whether to invest or not.

You should use a similar process when making any substantial strategic investments in your Eternity Portfolio. Here's another quote from Dr. Bright:

Don't be afraid to ask questions. Find out the condition of the "soil." Investigate the financial soundness and integrity of the organization soliciting your support; determine what percentage of your donation will actually go to the project and whether your gift will really be used for the glory of God.[2]

> Start the due diligence process as an investment, not a gift. You have to be sensitive to the leading of the Holy Spirit, and that leading trumps everything. However, often saying it's the Holy Spirit's leading is an excuse for lazy due diligence.
>
> *Larry Powell*

Your initial review should begin with the organization's promotional materials and financial statements. Spend some time going through its website to gain an overall understanding of what the ministry is about. Begin to write down questions and start to pray that God would guide your decision.

For larger investments, arrange a visit to the organization so you can meet with the leadership. (Try to go as high up the chain as possible; obviously this is easier with smaller organizations or if you are a very large donor.) The *time* you invest in this evaluation process should be in direct proportion to the *resources* you are going to invest. Throughout the process you should try to measure the organization on five major criteria: purpose, people, philosophy, process, and performance.

A more extensive checklist of questions is included in Appendix C to help you get started in the due diligence process, but let's briefly examine these five areas.

Purpose. From the moment of initial contact with the ministry you should receive a clear message about its reason for existence. Get some historical information. How was the organization founded? How long ago? Is it still doing what the founder envisioned? Review the mission and values statement. Is it compelling and focused or vague and broad? Does the purpose of this ministry match your personal mission priorities?

Does the organization exist merely to treat symptoms of a problem, or is it addressing root causes? Gordon MacDonald gives a great example of this using a twist on the story of the Good Samaritan. Most of us know the story: The Samaritan comes along the road to Jericho and sees a man beaten and bleeding, lying in the ditch—obviously a victim of the robbers and bandits who prey on travelers along that lonely road. The Samaritan has compassion on this man and takes him to a local inn for treatment, paying for the man's care out of his own money (Luke 10:30-37). Now what if the Good Samaritan came along that road again the following week and found another man in the same condition? And then the same thing happened the following week? At some point he should ask himself, "Should I continue paying for triage for the victims at the local inn, or should I invest in making this road a safer place?"

Similarly, as you look to make an investment, try to determine if the organization has a *strategic vision* for its role in accomplishing God's plan.

One major question you should always ask is "What makes this organization unique?" Among the hundreds of thousands of nonprofit organizations there is a good bit of overlap. Is someone already doing this same ministry in the same location? If so, maybe the two could join forces to achieve greater economies of scale. When it comes to investing dollars for the kingdom, you don't want an organization that is reinventing the wheel merely to paint it a new color.

Further to Alan's point, it's okay to ask an organization why they're the best one to fund in that space. They may give you a song and dance, but they also may have some concrete reasons and examples as to why you should fund them to tackle the issue at hand. This question becomes a helpful litmus test for whether organizations really know their stuff and how they're uniquely suited to get at a problem, or if they simply care but don't really stand out above the pack.

Heather Tuininga

> The best leaders are passionate about a cause but not blind to the fact that another organization may be better positioned or more capable.
>
> *Larry Powell*

People. Learn early in this process that you are investing in people, not ideas or organizations. Everything rises and falls on leaders and the teams they assemble. Those you meet within the organization should be passionate about what is going on and feel their work is crucial. If the leaders or staff are merely passing time or are halfhearted in their efforts, you don't need to conduct any further investigation.

What qualifications do they bring? What is their track record? After decades of investing in the kingdom, Hugh Maclellan describes his key leadership indicator this way: "Past successes are the best predictor of future successes." There will be exceptions, especially for those new to ministry, but inquire into the leaders' past work experience for clues. Do you get the sense that the head of the organization has a deep personal relationship with God and that he or she is a person on a mission?

> God seems to use certain people disproportionately. I want to invest with those types of leaders who have kingdom hearts and will make a disproportionate impact.
>
> *Jack Alexander*

Talk to board members if possible. (Do not consider investing in a ministry that does not have a board unless it is a startup and the board is under construction.) These individuals should know more about the strategic direction of the ministry than anyone besides the CEO. Are the board members invested financially? If not, you should question from the outset whether you should be either.

> Every organization needs money and a great board. Related to the board: How engaged are they? How much mindshare and engagement is the organization getting from them? How much do they give? Is there a spirit of unity but a diversity of thought? Are they serious about excellence? Are they supportive without being psychologically indebted to the founder/leadership?
>
> *Larry Powell*

Staff members are a thermometer to gauge the health of the organization. Are they busy? High-octane, leveraged organizations always have more to do than the existing staff can handle. At the same time, the staff should experience joy arising from a deep sense of purpose. Their attitudes and actions will reveal whether the lofty goals and vision of the organization are more than just snazzy marketing.

Philosophy. Each organization has its own way of doing things. Leadership greatly influences this defining philosophy, but it is also derived from the qualifications and personalities of the staff. Try to develop a feel for this by examining the ministry's approach to major functional areas.

Fundraising is an example. Does the ministry see it as a necessary evil or as a way to involve people in its work? Is the staff building long-term partnerships or "selling a product"? Are they creative? Richard Steckel writes, "A common characteristic of excellent nonprofit organizations is the presence of innovative strategies for income generation. These organizations are 'venture seekers,' meaning that they go actively looking for ideas to generate income and often seek out private sector businesses as partners."[3]

Is the ministry always in some sort of crisis fundraising mode (claiming, for example, "The lights will go off if we don't receive X number of dollars by the end of the month"), using emotional pleas to substitute for strategic, faith-based planning?

How does the leadership approach decision making? Do leaders implement unilateral, top-down mandates? Do they actively solicit planning input from staff and advisors? It is one thing to have a so-called open-door policy; it is an entirely different matter to *cultivate* a systematic process of including staff and volunteers in strategic planning.

Finally, is there a sense of accountability, both to God and His will, and to those who invest in the ministry? The most strategic ministries are transparent with both their successes and their failures. They view a donor as a valuable partner and prize his wisdom, prayers, *and* financial resources. Consider it a red flag if the organization is unwilling or reluctant to provide the information you request.

Process. How does the organization carry out its mission? Allowing for the early stages of a new ministry, investment-quality organizations have solid infrastructure and systems in place and working effectively. Is there a written strategic business plan? How are the main activities of ministry, management, and marketing being carried out? Is the organization tracking progress and working toward identifiable goals?

Dig into the financial situation. Where does the money come from? Does the ministry spend more money on fundraising than programs? Are the proper accounting systems in place with appropriate controls? Does an independent accounting firm conduct an audit each year?

Basically, you are trying to judge how effective the ministry is at its mission. Does it have the size, scope, and capacity to really push the ball forward, or will most of your investment be lost to inefficiencies? Once again, keep in mind that startup ministries will need time to ramp up. In those cases, spend as much time as possible with the leaders to determine their mind-set in this area. Leaders understand the value of building effective systems of operation.

Performance. Part of being a wise investment manager is periodic performance measurement. The question is basically "How has the ministry done?" Has it been effective at executing its game plan and achieving results? Evaluating performance is an ongoing part of managing your Eternity Portfolio, but you should consider it even before making the first investment. Remember, when analyzing new ministries, look at the track record of the leaders in their previous occupations. Do the same for board members. If there is no verifiable history of success, proceed with caution.

Performance is a tricky issue within nonprofits. Because of the nature of the business, it is often difficult to quantify success. The first step is for the organization to identify specific, measurable objectives. There will likely be a mixture of "activity-related" goals (e.g., "identify and meet with twenty potential church planters") and "mission-related" goals (e.g., "plant four hundred churches"). Both are important; however, over time, the ministry must place emphasis on achieving the main top-level mission goals.

An indicator of a truly strategic ministry is that each key staff person has individual, written objectives over the short and long term. Ask for examples of some goals that have been accomplished lately. How have things changed over time? Talk to people outside the organization, either indirectly related or in their target market. What is the perception of the organization? Is God glorified by the goals being accomplished as well as the way they are being accomplished?

> I want to understand how an organization measures success. It can be difficult to measure spiritual results, but you have to try. And you *can* measure inputs. I ask, "How do you know you're being a good steward of the money entrusted to you?"
> *Larry Powell*
>
> *[Author's note: Larry's question gets to the heart of his first point: wanting to be a good steward forces you to think about the best way to measure impact.]*

One final note about performance: *Allow proven leaders the latitude to take risks.* Those who are trying to stay on the forefront of God's leading are sure to make some mistakes along the way. It is in the nature of exploration that "dry wells" will be dug. Although you obviously do not want to see a pattern of major failures, as long as those in leadership are accountable, they should not be prohibited from exploring new territory. (Appendix C contains a checklist to which you can add your own comments and questions as you develop a feel for the due-diligence process.)

MAKING THE DECISION

After much prayer and research, you are finally ready to make a decision. You have invested considerable time and energy in evaluating a particular opportunity; now take a step back and look at the big picture. Ask yourself, *How well do I understand the leadership and the organization? Even if it is a great ministry, do I feel led specifically to be involved right now? Are there any red flags I can't seem to shake? What about my motives?*

167

Be careful there are no prideful or self-serving motives driving your investment. You might find it helpful to identify any potential conflicts of interest between your personal benefit and the Kingdom benefit. If there is some sort of personal benefit, perhaps you should give a hard second look to the whole thing. For example, are you trying to impress someone by your giving? Are you trying to create business or personal opportunities by giving? There may be times when you decide not to make an investment because you realize that the driving motivation was really your personal gratification.

How much to give and for how long can also be tricky decisions. With established organizations, you may want to try to fund specific projects. An example would be funding the translation of Scripture into a new language or training five hundred indigenous church planters in Asia. You may not be able to fund the whole project, but you could have a part. Successful donors want to make a measurable difference.

For long-term funding needs, consider establishing a defined time period for your investment. Once that time is over, you can reevaluate the investment opportunity to see if it still fits with God's will for your Eternity Portfolio. This allows the ministry to plan with no misunderstanding of your commitment.

If you're a major investor, be careful about funding too much of a ministry's operating budget. For example, foundations typically establish rules for how they support new organizations. (e.g., "no more than 25 percent of the operating budget for no more than three years"). If the ministry is really strategic, it should be able to attract more than one or two major investors over time.

> It is very easy for faith-based ministries to become too dependent on you. Therefore, from the outset it's good to encourage them to seek other relationships that could become supporters. The key to support is relationships!
>
> *Dr. Johnny Hunt*

One family foundation in the Seattle area has taken this concept [of shared funding] to heart and even put language on their website for organizations who want to apply for funds: "We will not fund more than 25% of a project/program, so as to leave room for other donors to experience the joy of giving to the project/program."

Heather Tuininga

HELPING WITHOUT HURTING

There is a dark side to giving that isn't often discussed except among those really serious about the call to generosity. The truth is that giving can sometimes be a problem—we can hurt people and whole communities by helping them. This dark side of generosity typically results from careless narcissism or clueless compassion. Both stem from the affluence of our society and, in many cases, a commendable desire to do good. The danger arises when I act as if *my doing good* is the most important part of the equation or when I believe that *because my intentions are good, the results must be good.* I hear people say, "God just told me to give; I can't worry about how they use it," or, "It's never wrong to give." I'm afraid that many times these are emotional responses from a moment of spiritual euphoria, guilt, or—dare I say it?—even self-righteousness.

Certainly we don't use the same action-without-accountability philosophy in our businesses or our families when raising children. We consider carefully how we undertake financial dealings in business and how we give to our families. We consider potential negative aspects, the impact to our children's worldviews, and so forth. Such thoughtfulness and intentionality needs to carry over

Continued on next page

into our giving strategies both domestically and in other countries. Gary Miller wrote in *The Other Side of the Wall:*

> When we continue to provide food, clothes, or shelter to people capable of providing for themselves, we sow the seeds of dependency, and we share in the blame for their condition. Most of us understand this concept in developed countries. We would not continue to feed an able-bodied son in bed or continue paying credit card bills for a brother who habitually makes poor choices. But when we go to underdeveloped countries, we tend to believe this principle doesn't apply. We compare their living conditions to our own and decide that continual relief is not only easier, it is also proper. We understand that welfare programs destroy incentive in our culture, but there is something else we need to understand: welfare doesn't work in theirs either.[4]

Gary's deep understanding of this problem comes from years of working with the poor through microfinance and microenterprise in Africa, Latin America, and Haiti.

Have you considered that your giving could actually make a problem worse? Many givers have not. But you would if you were Bob Lupton, founder of FCS Urban Ministries. Bob has spent more than forty years bringing together communities of resource with communities of need in the inner city of Atlanta. He's been serving up close and personal with many of the problems that plague urban America, including poverty, crime, and lack of education. He understands the needs and has successfully pioneered many solutions. But Bob's latest book, *Toxic Charity,* is directed at those who would help, educating givers about the dangers of insensitivity, patronizing behavior, and often blissful ignorance that characterize so much well-meaning effort in the Christian community. Bob writes:

> The compassion industry is almost universally accepted as a virtuous and constructive enterprise. But what is so surprising is that its outcomes are almost entirely unexamined. The food we ship to Haiti, the well we dig in Sudan, the clothes we distribute in inner-city Detroit—all seem like such worthy efforts. Yet those closest to the ground—on the receiving end of this outpouring of generosity—quietly admit that it may be hurting more than helping. How? Dependency. Destroying personal initiative. When we do for those in need what they have the capacity to do for themselves, we disempower them.[5]

For Brian Fikkert, working in international relief and development revealed that the "toxic charity" problem affects both the *giver and the recipient.*

"One of the biggest problems in many poverty-alleviation efforts is that their design and implementation exacerbates the poverty of being of the economically rich—their god-complexes—and the poverty of being of the economically poor—their feelings of inferiority and shame."[6]

His groundbreaking book *When Helping Hurts* delves deeply into the spiritual roots of poverty and the spiritual dangers that easily entangle those who would help.

"Poverty is the result of relationships that do not work, that are not just, that are not for life, that are not harmonious or enjoyable," he writes. "Poverty is the absence of shalom in all its meanings."[7] Fikkert, a professor with

Continued on next page

a Ph.D. in economics from Yale University, is the founder and president of the Chalmers Center at Covenant College. He specializes in international economics and economic development. Most of us sense that poverty is not primarily (or at least perpetually) a money problem. But Fikkert and co-writer Steve Corbett provide a practical as well as theological and academic framework for addressing it.

Assessing root issues

It's important that we spend the time to assess root problems and not just allocate resources to alleviate symptoms. Assessing the root issue is a continuous learning process—and critical for creating lasting change.

> When a sick person goes to the doctor, the doctor could make two crucial mistakes: (1) Treating symptoms instead of the underlying illness; (2) Misdiagnosing the underlying illness and prescribing the wrong medicine. Either one of these mistakes will result in the patient not getting better and possibly getting worse. The same is true when we work with poor people. If we treat only the symptoms or if we misdiagnose the underlying problem, we will not improve their situation, and we might actually make their lives worse.[8]

Thoughtful investors and the best charitable organizations analyze, early on, various situations to evaluate whether the problems call for relief, for rehabilitation, or for development.

> Rushing in to rescue victims from calamity may be the very highest and noblest of acts. Partnering and investing with those entrapped in chronic need is

an equally noble response. Wisdom is required to determine which is the more appropriate course in each particular case. . . . When relief does not transition to development in a timely way, compassion becomes toxic.[9]

Six basic questions can help assess problems and appropriate responses:
1. Did the situation happen suddenly?
2. Do they lack physical or mental ability?
3. Will they be harmed if I do nothing?
4. Do they lack basic resources?
5. Were they using good management skills?
6. Is this the first attempt to help?[10]

If the answers to these six questions are yes, writes Gary Miller, then the need is "critical," calling for relief, such as food, shelter, and clothing. If answers are no, then the need probably falls into a "chronic" category, calling for opportunity, rehabilitation, and development.[11]

The temptation, of course, is to fall back on relief. "We like to fix things fast," writes Miller, "and sustainable solutions take time—sometimes a lot of time."[12] For example, many people who have grown up in poverty are acclimated to begging or receiving as part of life. No one ever helped them to grow their abilities. Certainly changing long-ingrained patterns "take teaching and time, but the potential results are worth striving for. Continuing a handout is less kind than moving toward developing opportunities and skills."[13]

Retain a focus on Christ
Another giving pitfall is to move ahead enthusiastically
Continued on next page

with projects that may alleviate poverty and suffering but that don't include the good news about Jesus. After all, the biggest, deepest need of every human being is to find a relationship with his or her Creator. Jesus is the whole answer—for body, soul, and spirit.

> Too often we drill wells, dispense medicine, and provide food without narrating that Jesus Christ is the Creator and Provider of these material things. Then later we offer a Bible study in which we explain that Jesus can save our souls. This approach communicates evangelical Gnosticism: material things solve material poverty, and Jesus solves spiritual poverty. In other words, we communicate "Star Trek Jesus" rather than "Colossians 1 Jesus." As a result, we fail to introduce materially poor people to the only one who can truly reconcile the broken relationships that underlie their material poverty.[14]

Christians need to balance and blend the kind of help they offer, not ignoring the urgency of physical needs, either. It makes sense to alleviate the pressing needs of hunger and disease. After all, how can people think about the state of their souls with the distraction of constant hunger pains? But Christians will recognize the issue of our broken relationship with God as an underlying root cause they also must address.

> Without addressing sin, we are only applying a bandage to cover the problem. This is one of the reasons humanitarian aid has fallen into disrepute among some believers. They see individuals and organizations trying to make the world a better place without dealing with the source of the problem, and

these believers overreact by deciding that physical aid is a waste of precious resources and time. You will not find this response or reaction in the life of Jesus, though. Jesus didn't shy away from helping people physically. He spent much of His time meeting their natural needs, and there is still a call for His people to help physically, even as they point others to Jesus.[15]

Avoid condescension and paternalism

Those in the giving position can sometimes look down on those who must, of necessity, receive. But it's a mistake to think that those who lack material wealth don't have wisdom or spiritual insight to offer. Fikkert writes about his realization that those who are needy often have a deeper faith and connection to God.

> As I listened to these people praying to be able to live another day, I thought about my ample salary, my life insurance policy, my health insurance policy, my two cars, my house, etc. I realized that I do not really trust in God's sovereignty on a daily basis, as I have sufficient buffers in place to shield me from most economic shocks. I realized that when these folks pray the fourth petition of the Lord's prayer— Give us this day our daily bread—their minds do not wander as mine does. I realized that while I have sufficient education and training to deliver a sermon on God's sovereignty with no forewarning, these slum dwellers were trusting in God's sovereignty just to get them through the day. And I realized that these people had a far deeper intimacy with God than I probably will ever have in my entire life.[16]

Continued on next page

One aspect of treating the recipients of our giving with dignity is allowing them to be part of the solution. God built into his orderly world a system with incentives that shape us productively. We learn to enjoy the rewarding feeling of working to provide for ourselves and those we love. *"Solutions must cost . . . something,"* Miller writes.

> When dealing with ongoing need, the one being blessed needs to bear the majority of the burden. Effective help provides what they can't, but never what they can. This is difficult because we assume there is little they can do. But search for ways they can repay what they receive. This not only helps them believe they are capable, it also teaches them to give back to their community.[17]

When both donors and recipients of the gifts share in the investment of a certain project, then failure has shared consequences. If the recipients know the giving investors will swoop in to save the day, their participation may lack drive and enthusiasm.

> Fear of failure is a wonderful motivator. When we remove that and insulate a person from all cost, we ask for failure. As soon as anyone learns, whether locally or in a foreign country, that you will pick up the tab if things don't work out, then be prepared to start picking up tabs. If a program is to be truly sustainable, it can't depend solely on us.[18]

The point is to empower those in need—not to *disempower* them through good-hearted yet misguided giving. "Giving to those in need what they could be gaining from their own initiative may well be the kindest way to destroy people," writes Robert Lupton in *Toxic Charity*.[19]

Paternalism means treating others as if they're your children and are unable to grow up. The goal for parents should be to enable their kids, over time, to function as independent adults. If parents stunt that process by overprotection or overprovision, they undermine the process. Miller writes:

> One of the most challenging aspects of working with the poor is the reality that I am shaping their thinking regarding themselves. . . . Be very careful what you think about the poor. . . . If you think they are hopeless and helpless, then you will probably head down the paternalistic road, and before long they will begin to think of themselves as hopeless and helpless as well. But if you can see them as fellow children of God with abilities and local resources that they can utilize to provide for themselves, they will begin to think of themselves the same way. And as they begin to focus on and develop the resources God has placed in their care, real change can begin to occur.[20]

Helping without hurting requires a lot of humility. Donors must somehow put themselves in the world and experiences of the beneficiary.

Larry Powell

One writer refers to the plight of the needy as a "struggle for self-sufficiency" that is "an essential

Continued on next page

strength-building process that should not be short-circuited by 'compassionate' intervention. The effective helper can be an encourager, a coach, a partner, but never a caretaker."[21] Be on the lookout for paternalism in all its forms. As Corbett and Fikkert write, these can include resource paternalism, spiritual paternalism, knowledge paternalism, labor paternalism, and managerial paternalism.

If I could ask Jesus just one question about giving, it would be, "Where does love end and improper codependency begin?" It's such a blurry area where grace and mercy collide with truth, and it should be a struggle for us. God's heart is bent toward mercy, and that's how I want to be bent—but not to the point where I ignore warning signs that my giving is creating a problem.

Jack Alexander

The path becomes clearer as we think through our motives to the real objective.
Because your Eternity Portfolio is about building God's kingdom and not building your own self-worth or self-interest, you'll find yourself double-checking your motives—and then double-checking them again! Sorting out your motivations is hard, but it allows you to think clearly about real solutions—and not kid yourself about quick fixes. Corbett and Fikkert ask, "Do you really love poor people and want to serve them? Or do you have other motives? I confess to you that part of what motivates me to help the poor is my felt need to accomplish something worthwhile with my life, to be a person of significance, to feel like I have pursued a noble cause."[22]

In his book *Toxic Charity,* Bob Lupton explains the difference between "evaluating our charity by the *rewards we receive through service* rather than the benefits received by the served."[23] Our due diligence needs to be focused on the work that's accomplished and the people who are helped—and not focused on the benefit to ourselves as givers.

There are many causes and conditions of poverty, including lack of basic necessities, ignorance, social injustice, and spiritual condition. Fixing any one of them won't necessarily solve the problem. As God leads, He will probably call us to do something, but it starts with being humble regarding the complexities involved. Physicians take an oath promising to "do no harm." That's a good starting point. Then we proceed slowly and continuously evaluate results, particularly results of those who've made similar attempts before you. Why has this problem not been fixed before? Have others tried and failed for reasons I've not considered yet? What makes me think my solution will have a different outcome?

The idea that you can do harm with good intentions is very real but most people don't think anything about it. Being a true steward requires taking some responsibility for the results as well as the gift.

Larry Powell

So we pursue methodical thoughtfulness, prayerfulness, and humility—trying to understand what our Father would want in our service to those we would help. Bob Lupton helps us clarify this deeper connection between actions and best outcomes.

> If we cared about, for instance, seeing human dignity enhanced, or trusting relationships being formed, or self-sufficiency increasing, then we could employ proven methods known to accomplish these goals. We know that trust grows with accountability over time. We know that mutual exchange and legitimate negotiating is energizing (people of every culture love to bargain!). And we know that employment starts people on the path to self-reliance. We know these things. And we have the capacity to accomplish them.[24]

INVITATIONS TO JOIN THE BOARD

One final area of interest when making wise investments concerns the board of directors. If you are considering a sizeable investment, do not be surprised if your due diligence process generates an offer to serve on the board of directors of the organization. As you become known to ministry leaders, your services will be in demand—and rightfully so. There is a need for godly, engaged, strategic thinkers to assist ministries at the board level. As you consider such opportunities, keep several things in mind.

There is an old saying that the board of directors is needed for the three Ws—wealth, wisdom, and work. My experience in working with ministry leaders is that wealth (and relationships with others who have it) tends to be the most desired of the three! However, the most effective organizations use the varied skills and experience of their board members. When the board is truly engaged as a body of accountability and strategic planning, the members become the best mouthpieces of the ministry. Some on the board will be great at fundraising, others will be best at planning, still others will be good at building strategic partnerships with other organizations and individuals. All are needed.

Before you commit to serving on a board, ask questions of the ministry leader. Make sure you know what the organization will expect of you as a board member. Are you responsible for a certain amount of fundraising? How much time will be required? Are the meetings for actual planning and strategizing, or merely for rubber-stamping the director's plans? A good understanding is critical to a good decision. Ask the hard questions now or you may find yourself in an awkward situation later, when expectations are unfulfilled on both sides. When there is a good fit, however, nothing is more fulfilling than being able to assist a ministry with your time and talents as well as your financial resources. Don't underestimate the difference you could make personally.

THE ETERNITY PORTFOLIO INVESTMENT POLICY STATEMENT

Thomas Edison once said that genius is 1 percent inspiration and 99 percent perspiration. Part of the perspiration comes from trying to remember the vague details of an incredible idea you worked out two weeks ago in a short burst of inspiration. The best-laid plans are *wasted* without proper documentation.

In the world of investing for institutions and high-net-worth individuals, it is common practice to work out a written agreement documenting how a portfolio will be managed. Often called an investment policy statement, this document is intended to accomplish four main goals:

- Establish expectations for and objectives of the portfolio
- Outline the responsibilities of all parties
- Provide guidelines for carrying out the plan
- Communicate benchmarks for evaluating performance

The investment policy statement serves to document the game plan and hold each party accountable for his or her part in the process. The statement should be reviewed on a regular basis to determine if it needs to be changed—whether in the strategy itself or in the execution. Without a well-documented plan, the investment portfolio is likely to drift from its core objectives and become less effective.

Your Eternity Portfolio strategy is no exception. Once you spend the time to work out your plan, don't waste that effort through forgetfulness or a lack of accountability. An Eternity Portfolio investment policy statement could be an integral part of your family's ongoing giving strategy. (Appendix B has an example of an Eternity Portfolio investment policy statement.)

You can customize the policy statement to suit your particular situation, but you will probably want to cover at least the following major points:

1. **Mission Statement.** Lay out the guiding principles for your Eternity Portfolio. This can be as simple as defining the major focus areas and types of investments you are contemplating. As God works in your life over the years, expect your mission to become further refined and focused.

2. **Funding Strategy.** Document your planned investing method, including amounts and timing as well as any special funding vehicles (e.g., trusts, foundations, donor-advised funds). You may also want to include some financial projections that illustrate how you arrived at the numbers.

3. **Investment Selection.** Outline the steps you've taken to evaluate potential investments. It may be helpful to include a standard due diligence checklist such as the one shown in Appendix C.

4. **Implementation.** This section should include a list of the organizations currently supported within the portfolio and the estimated amount or percentage you plan to invest in each.

5. **Ongoing Monitoring.** Describe the steps that you will take (and with what frequency) to ensure that organizations funded by the portfolio are using resources effectively to accomplish the mission.

Review the policy statement on a regular basis to make sure it is still in alignment with your family's desires. This can be a great time for teaching children and grandchildren about the importance of giving. As they see your commitment to serving and helping others through proactive planning, that vision increases in their young hearts. It is never too early to emphasize the importance of investing in the kingdom of God, and your annual Eternity Portfolio meetings can provide the opportunity.

Another benefit of family involvement is the chance to communicate your specific investing values to the next generation. This becomes important in the case of a private foundation that transcends the death of its founder. The more your heirs understand about your giving values, the greater the chance that your wishes will be respected after you are gone.

> [Monitoring donor organizations is] not just a great time for teaching, but also a time to share the delight and joy of being involved in God's kingdom work through intentional generosity!
>
> *Todd Harper*

> At some point in the initial process it is a good idea to ask: "How much involvement should the younger generations have in *creating the plan*?"
>
> *David Wills*

MAINTAIN ACCOUNTABILITY

We started this chapter by talking about two types of accountability. First, as stewards, we are accountable to God for our eternal investments. Rather than giving haphazardly, we should be seeking God's direction and using His wisdom to make wise investments.

Second, we should require accountability within our specific investments. No longer should we give money and then simply forget about the results. For organizations you support with sizeable investments on an ongoing basis, schedule regular annual or semiannual meetings with leadership to stay updated. If this isn't possible, make sure you read the organization's newsletter or website updates and ask questions. Find out what has gone well since the last meeting and where the difficulties lie. These meetings are the perfect opportunity to offer nonfinancial support in the way of prayer or actual participation in the ministry's work.

In the case of special grants, set a follow-up meeting to discuss the results of the project. Was it an effective use of funds? How can it be done even better next time?

What you will find over time is that the most strategic ministries will communicate proactively with their investment partners. They may not know how at first, but you could be instrumental in helping define what good communication looks like. When you first get involved, offer suggestions about the kind of performance feedback you would like. Strategic organizations value donors as people, not merely as funding sources.

Remember, the word is *accountability*. Those with a long-term view for success realize that God made us to work together, not to be lone rangers. Accountability drives open communication, fulfilled expectations, and ultimately greater effectiveness in ministry. Settle for nothing less, and vote with your investment dollars.

Figure out the key measurements you want to monitor and ask for those up front, and again as you check in periodically. Other good monitoring questions:

- How many people were impacted?

- Did the project come in on budget? If not, please explain.

- Did you learn any lessons or face any challenges/barriers with the program? If so, how did you handle the challenges, and will the lessons learned inform your future work?

- If your program is ongoing, how are your plans for sustainability progressing?

- Will the project bring about long-lasting change for those you serve? If so, please elaborate. If not, why?

- Please describe your goals for the upcoming year of the project/program and how those goals capitalize on or are different from the objectives you initially set for the project/program.

Heather Tuininga

In addition to maintaining accountability, there will be times when we should maintain anonymity. In Matthew 6:3, Jesus says, "But when you give to the needy, do not let your left hand know what your right hand is doing, so that your giving may be in secret. Then, your Father who sees what is done in secret will reward you." Money can be used to exert control in relationships. We need to be generous but also be sensitive to how our resources might affect our relationships with the poor and vulnerable.

Jack Alexander

KINGDOM ENTERPRISE IS TAKING NEW FORMS

Have you heard of an *L3C organization*, or a *B corp*? How about *impact investing* or *social enterprise*? These new concepts are changing the face of philanthropy—particularly for affluent families and established foundations. The core idea is a hybrid structure and philosophy (for profit/not for profit) to more effectively achieve a nonfinancial mission. For Christians, the opportunities are expanding to combine the best of business and free enterprise with the best of charity in order to accomplish kingdom purposes. Sustainability and scale are two key reasons for the new developments. In general, an organization that can accomplish its purpose through revenue generation within its target market (versus ongoing donations) is more sustainable. Further, a growing ecosystem of such organizations can be nurtured and sustained to create an exponential impact with scale that would not be possible through traditional charitable funding. More capacity and more appropriate legal structures bring even greater financial resources to bear from pools of capital not accessible to most traditional charitable organizations. These "impact investments" are appropriate for the investor looking for a social or kingdom return on investment as a primary motivation (where financial returns are a factor, but only a secondary one, with financial returns often expected to be below market rates).

For instance, one company creates and sells an inexpensive solar lighting system that seems just right to meet the needs of hundreds of millions of families around the world who lack access to reliable electrical power. Many rely on open fires that not only generate poor lighting but also increase health risks, especially to children, from

Continued on next page

burns and pollution. The founder recognized the potential to enhance health, education, and working conditions by creating a low-cost, solar-powered system. This company's particular challenge is to manufacture a product that is affordable for consumers at the base of the global income pyramid while still generating enough revenue to make the organization viable. Impact investments may fund the initial startup, research and development, or an expansion phase. But the enterprise is designed and managed to sustain itself on product revenue over the long term while serving the materially poor as its primary motive. The structure and aligned objectives of the impact investors allow the organization to eliminate or reduce profit *distributions* so that more dollars can be directed toward the mission.

Legal structures are important in these new forms of investment, particularly for regulated organizations such as private foundations. For example, the primary reason for the new L3C (low-profit, limited liability corporation) organizations is to meet IRS requirements for "program-related investments." Much of the law in western countries requires a fiduciary duty of managers to put the interests of owners and shareholders first in running a business. And that typically resolves in a profitability emphasis. The new structures spell out nonfinancial objectives (i.e., social benefit) as a proper emphasis, even if it means lower profit.

Not all charitable missions lend themselves to these new forms—in fact, some of the most pressing needs (e.g., crisis relief efforts) require conventional forms of generosity by definition. Even for those organizations where a business orientation seems appropriate, it's not easy to generate the financial results that make a sustainable enterprise. Remember, operating at breakeven (zero profits) is not sustainable. Even without an explicit profit motive, an organization has to generate "net income" over time and sow it back into the business to meet the needs of the future, or it will have to raise funds externally to meet those needs.

DISCUSSION QUESTIONS

1. In the past, how have you decided which organizations to support? Do you know how effective they were in using your money?

2. Have you ever thought about your responsibility for what happens *after* you give money to an organization? Do you think you hold any responsibility for this?

3. Consider the organizations or individuals in which you are investing today. How do they measure up based on the information in this chapter?

4. Do you think it's possible you may be called to invest in an organization that, based on earthly wisdom and prudence, just does not measure up well? Why or why not?

5. How do you find a balance between accountability for your investments and faith?

6. What is your reaction to creating an Eternity Portfolio investment policy statement? How might it help or hinder your giving?

Passing the Baton: A Legacy That Outlasts You

- What will be your living legacy?
- What about a financial legacy?
- Planning your children's inheritance
- Tools and techniques for advanced philanthropy

D r. James Dobson, a psychologist and foremost expert on the family, compares the transfer of values to a relay: the most hazardous part of the competition is the handoff. At three different times during the race, a sprinting athlete, at the peak of his effort in the competition, must hand the baton to the next runner, who is just getting started. If there is a collision, the race is lost. If one runner drops the baton, the race is lost. Even if the runners transfer the baton successfully, if it is not done smoothly and efficiently, the race may be lost. The athletes must practice the handoff over and over to succeed at the highest level.

Dr. Dobson believes that in raising a Christian family, the biggest opportunity for failure is in the handoff—the transfer of values to the next generation. Although much can be learned through experience, it is parents' and teachers' intentional training that will give children the biblically based understanding they need to achieve success.

You may already be "running well" from the perspective of your Eternity Portfolio. Or perhaps you are just getting started. If you are faithful to invest for the kingdom during this lifetime, your reward will be great. But there is something bigger. *Start thinking now about finishing well so that you create a legacy that outlasts you.*

You have the ability to influence future generations in two specific ways so that, even after you are gone from this earth, you can continue to invest until the end of time. First, you can create a *living legacy* of people you have trained and influenced to create their own Eternity Portfolios. Second, you may be able to leave a *financial legacy* that will continue to make actual monetary investments after you're gone.

THE GREATEST OPPORTUNITY—A LIVING LEGACY

You might think the only way to leave a legacy is by virtue of a massive financial fortune accumulated over a lifetime. Although we will discuss opportunities to use wealth in this way, the *highest* return potential actually has little to do with the dollars you leave. Training others to be faithful managers offers a greater reward because in some way you will share in the rewards of their efforts.

God has called me to disciple others in faithful life management, and that is one of the reasons for this book. If just a fraction of those who read it catch the vision and understand through Scripture God's plan for their life and the incredible opportunity of investing in eternity, the leverage will be incredible. The same volume of leverage occurs with other teachers and pastors. And, while we are not all called to be teachers outside the home, those of us with children *are* called to be their teachers. This is where we have the best opportunity to create a living legacy as we pass along the baton of financial faithfulness. How should we go about this crucial task?[1]

> One of my life's callings has been that of mentoring young Christians and leaders. I believe prayer and then modeling generosity is most effective. Great truths are caught as well as taught. What's important to you will become important to those you mentor. "It's not the what you know but the truth you live, that is most appealing and effective."
>
> *Dr. Johnny Hunt*

A LIVING LEGACY BEGINS WITH COMMUNICATION

The transfer of values is most successful when there is early, frequent, and ongoing communication. What people learn in childhood stays with them forever. As God gave the law to Moses and the nation of Israel, He instructed them about their responsibility to the next generation.

> And these words which I command you today shall be in
> your heart. You shall teach them diligently to your children,
> and shall talk of them when you sit in your house, when you
> walk by the way, when you lie down, and when you rise up.
> (Deuteronomy 6:6–7)

Lay the foundation with Scripture. The central focus of all teaching should be God's Word, the Bible. Remember that only God has the power to shape a child's (or an adult's!) heart. He is responsible for life change.

When it comes to teaching faithful stewardship, focus on the verses that give instruction in that area. Help your children get a big vision for God and His plan for all of creation. Without specific instruction in this area it is easy to develop a view of Christianity as a "Sunday thing," with associated rules and restrictions. Give your children a sense that as Christians, they are a part of God's plan—part of something much bigger than themselves.

Look for passages of Scripture that communicate God's heart for giving. Teach the connection between money given and lives changed through the gospel, discipleship, mercy, and justice. Highlight examples of generous people throughout the Bible and as you come across them in daily living. Show them short videos from trusted resources like GenerousGiving.org. Pray regularly that God will cultivate a heart of generosity in your children.

A LIVING LEGACY IS BUILT ON YOUR EXAMPLE

A faithful life is the best platform for teaching others. We all know that children learn by example. This is particularly true with giving; children of generous givers become generous givers, often because of the example they witnessed growing up. It has been said that you only believe as much of the Bible as you live day to day. Do not expect your children to believe what they don't see in your life. The faithful manager radiates the joy of the generous life in such a way as to be unbelievably attractive to others.

Tell your children about your Eternity Portfolio strategy and share stories of how you got to this point. What types of ministries make up your portfolio today? Why do you consider them strategic? Allow your children to share the experience. If you have grown children, plan special family events to gather and share how God has blessed you and what you are doing in light of that.

You don't need a lot of money to do this! I heard a story recently of a man who grew up in a poor family but whose father was particularly intentional about setting an example of giving. Every two weeks as he received his paycheck, the father would gather the family together to write out the "giving checks." They would pray together, thanking God for supplying their needs once again and asking His blessing on those they supported. What an example! It left an indelible mark on those children.

The most powerful story you can share with your children is what God is doing in your life. Live and share the standard you hope they will exceed. And don't forget, they are watching how you use *all* of your money, not just the part you give away.

> When our children were younger, I was very concerned about how our lifestyle decisions impacted their view of the world. We're sending a message to our kids about values, and we want to be really intentional about that message.
>
> *Larry Powell*

A LIVING LEGACY IS LEARNED BY EXPERIENCE

People learn by doing. Starting from the time they first receive an allowance or get paid for odd jobs, children should be taught to give. When my children were very young, they really did not even understand why they were giving away part of their allowance, but they enjoyed putting offerings in the plate at church. (I suspect this was due not so much to their generous nature but to the fact that they had very few "wants" not provided by their parents, so the value of money was not well understood!) With proper teaching and God's grace, giving that is learned as a discipline will grow into a more developed understanding.

Kids can learn a tremendous amount through helping the poor and homeless. Consider taking some "vision trips" to urban areas or, if your budget permits, to developing countries so your children can see how most of the world's population lives.

One of my major concerns for our children is that they understand how different their financial situation is from that of most people alive today. Although they may live in a middle-class world by American standards, that standard of living would easily be considered to be in the top 1% globally.

Seeing and helping those less fortunate will encourage your children to have hearts of gratitude and compassion. Let them experience firsthand the joy of passing along God's blessings. They can also assist in evaluating giving opportunities. Teach them the wisdom you have gained through developing your Eternity Portfolio investment policy statement. Allow them to participate in the planning over time.

For those who establish private foundations or other major financial legacies, it is even more critical to train up the next generation to be effective in making ministry investments. Consider including your children on the distribution committee to involve them in the process.

CAN YOU TRULY GIVE WHAT YOU'VE NEVER OWNED?
Despite years of experience and observation, I continue to wrestle with the question of how best to inspire and train the next generations in generosity. I'm thinking about two situations specifically: (1) multigenerational wealth, where the money was earned in the first generation and future generations are being trained to steward it, and (2) generous givers who don't have (or plan to continue) multigenerational wealth but nonetheless want their children and grandchildren to "catch the bug" of generosity and be wise givers in their own right.

There are a growing number of educational resources geared specifically to solid philanthropy technique, and I do think parental modeling, great training tools, and relevant experience are keys to wisdom in this process. But what about the heart of the giver? How do we inspire a generous spirit? Each young person is different, but we need to look for signs that generosity extends beyond

Continued on next page

effective distribution of the "family money." Many of the ways I've seen parents teaching generosity don't cost the kids anything that they really feel—in fact, sometimes it's just an abstract task that has to be completed at the family meeting. Generosity can't be forced as if learning algebra. And if generosity is truly taking hold, there should be evidence of personal sacrifice, of giving something up.

True giving has to do with the concept of ownership. Until I experience what it is like to own something that I could keep for myself and then decide to give it away, I haven't truly experienced generosity. *I can't give what I've never owned.* Apply this to our children and you get the nuance of what makes this challenging. Young people may not develop a heart of generosity if what they give is just Mom's and Dad's money. If we bring them along too quickly, young adults can become expert—even prideful—at giving away other people's money without experiencing the transforming power of true generosity in their own lives! Or they become resentful of being forced to participate in a process that doesn't really concern them, or worse, seems counter to their own interests. God owns it all, but He gives us certain elements of the ownership experience. These are the elements we need our children to *feel* (for example, as relates to their own money) so they can know what it means to wrestle with self and then experience the freedom and joy of generosity.

CONSIDER A FINANCIAL LEGACY

It is not difficult to think of people who have made a significant financial contribution to the welfare of society through their charitable giving. Andrew Carnegie, John Rockefeller, Bill and Melinda Gates, and others come quickly to mind. These individuals designed the framework of the legacy they would leave with their money. Not everyone has that opportunity (or, as Carnegie would tell you, that *burden*), but for those with significant financial resources it deserves careful consideration.

During your lifetime and after your death, you can take advantage of techniques to invest in your Eternity Portfolio while at the same time creating income and estate tax benefits. These techniques also focus and give structure to your philanthropic efforts.

When it comes to dividing the wealth you have accumulated, there are two categories of "voluntary" beneficiaries and one "involuntary" beneficiary to consider. Family and charitable beneficiaries I consider voluntary. As you may have guessed, government taxing authorities are the uninvited guests at the table who tend to be very well fed due to improper planning.

> During our lifetime we all pay "social capital"—taxes our governments use to do social programs, etc. At the end of life, again most of us will pay "social capital." The question is, Do you want to "self direct" your social capital (give it to charity of your choice), or do you want to let our governments direct your social capital? By planning ahead and giving to charity, you can direct your social capital.
>
> *Lorne Jackson*

Tax savings are a huge motivator in the area of planned giving. Many people make significant gifts in years when they have a large sale of stock or a business, retirement-plan payouts, or stock-option exercises, simply because of the income-tax savings. Certainly those are not the only times to consider a major investment in your Eternity Portfolio; however, any time you anticipate an extraordinary income-tax liability you should revisit your charitable-giving plan in the interest of good stewardship. You may wish to review the discussion in chapter 4 about income taxes.

The estate and gift tax is another matter altogether. This is basically the "transfer tax" on passing an inheritance to your family (other than your spouse). Although recently there have been attempts to reduce or even eliminate this tax, it is unlikely ever to go away for good. The bottom line is that, subject to certain lifetime exemptions, you pay a tax on major transfers to your family. Depending on your country and circumstances, it's not unusual for the marginal tax rate to be 50 percent or more. That means it could cost you a dollar in taxes to transfer a dollar to your children! Keep that in mind as we discuss leaving an inheritance for your children. If you have questions on the estate and gift tax, contact a tax advisor.

PLANNING YOUR CHILDREN'S INHERITANCE

What is the right amount to leave my children? Should I give it to them now or after my death? Should they all inherit equally? Whole books have been written to address the issue of inheritance. There are no easy answers, so instead let me propose a series of ten questions you should consider as you seek God's will for this area of your financial life:

1. What are we trying to accomplish by bestowing this inheritance on our children?
2. Do any of the children need an inheritance to provide care for physical or mental limitations?
3. Will the amount we plan to give be a hindrance to our children's proper character and spiritual development?
4. Do our children understand and practice faithful life management?
5. Is this inheritance going to further God's purpose in their lives?
6. Have we passed along life values as well as the inheritance?
7. Have we spent a considerable amount of time in prayer and study of Scripture to determine God's will for each child?
8. Are there educational needs of our children or grandchildren to be provided for?
9. Is it likely that this inheritance will create a dysfunctional work ethic or family dynamic?
10. Will the kingdom of God be advanced by virtue of this inheritance?

The Bible teaches that it is imperative to provide for one's family (see 1 Timothy 5:8), and it is good to leave an inheritance (see Proverbs 13:22). However, at some level, it can be overdone. When you consider the miserable success rate for people who inherit significant wealth, you begin to seriously question the level at which money can be a deadly inheritance.

For the sake of your children and grandchildren, tread cautiously.

A GOOD INHERITANCE:
WHAT MAKES THIS A HARD QUESTION?

For most people, leaving an "over-inheritance" is not a problem. For example, an estate that would enable the surviving children to own houses free of debt—a reasonable and powerful legacy—is actually beyond the capacity for most parents (without large life insurance policies). Above those levels is where it gets much more complicated. The thoughtful parent must prayerfully consider issues such as motivation, abilities, adverse incentives, training, and calling in determining God's will for the distribution of *His* assets.

We all want to bless our children. Personally, I have found the desire to give them things is almost overwhelming. Almost. The reason I can resist is that I've witnessed so many examples of how it goes wrong. The relationship between parent and child, the control issues, the unmet expectations, the myriad forms of entitlement, the bitterness. These are just a handful of the symptoms. When the dollars are big, the problems rise exponentially. It was not empty musing that prompted Andrew Carnegie to ask, "Why should men leave great fortunes to their children? If this is done from affection, is it not misguided affection? Observation teaches that, generally speaking, it is not well for the children that they should be so burdened."[2] Without prayer, proper training, and thoughtful deliberation, I submit that leaving *any* amounts that could alter a child's lifestyle or vocation is a mistake. Carnegie labeled it well: *misguided affection.*

However, if God has entrusted you with a large estate, you must wrestle with the issues for one simple reason: *Somebody has to manage the capital.* Think about that for a bit and you grasp the magnitude. Chances are the

Continued on next page

government will be managing a large portion when taxes are paid. Then, if you leave charitable bequests, the charitable organizations will be managing that portion. Whatever you leave to your kids will be managed by them. What distribution will bring God glory and further His kingdom objectives? Not an easy question.

What if you have a family business? It might make the most sense for one of your children, with proper training, to lead the business forward into future generations. This may also be best for a family foundation. In the decision process, I believe there is one question that stands out above all others. This is the bright light for illuminating your path: *What is my motivation for leaving this amount and form of inheritance?* Ask it again—and again and again. Don't allow rationalizations and mushy thinking to cloud the way God would speak to you. I would strongly challenge any result that makes my kids financially independent. Notice I didn't say to question the objective of making them financially independent. (Except in the case of health disabilities or for a specific season of time, my professional opinion is that having the *objective* of making your kids financially independent is generally a bad idea.) I mean strongly challenge any *result* that makes this happen—even if they are wise with money, even if they are seeking to follow Christ with their lives. Unearned financial freedom disconnects them from one of the strongest mechanisms of discerning God's will—the provision of daily resources. And you might be surprised how little "free money" it takes to cause a child to disconnect for years (and maybe decades) from a productive, Christ-honoring path. It always sounds innocuous, even spiritual—*giving them the freedom to really explore God's calling, do ministry, and the list goes on.* It is well-intentioned, and if we lived in a perfect world, it would turn out that way. But we don't. Misguided affection can be toxic, even with the best of intentions. And your good feelings about giving them money can fade quickly while the damage lasts. These are your children (and their spouses! And your grandchildren!), so go slowly and be careful.

It's safer to start with the default assumption that God entrusted you with the resources to steward (and possibly invest fully in His kingdom) through your lifetime. Safer to raise your children expecting to have to seek God and make their way in the world by His provision and their hard work. Start there and then consider what might empower them at the right level. You'll probably be doing this planning process at a time when they could use assistance currently with education or business opportunities. With increasing longevity these days, the most productive inheritance might be what you can do during your lifetime.

Although it is good to leave some inheritance to your children, remember that an inheritance is about much more than just a pot of money. In today's society, a discerning, biblical worldview along with critical thinking skills, education, and a solid work ethic may be the most valuable inheritance you leave.

CHARITABLE PLANNED GIVING

The simplest ways are not always best. As you consider the lifetime funding of your Eternity Portfolio, the simplest way is to give cash, as the resources are available, to the organizations you would like to benefit. But what if you would like to make a commitment to give and would like to save some taxes, but you also need to live on the income from your assets for the next twenty years? What if your only significant asset is a block of appreciated stock? What if you just sold your business and have one year to use a really large tax deduction but don't know when or where you would like to contribute that large sum?

You don't have to be a millionaire to benefit from planned giving. You can employ advanced giving strategies even if you only have a few thousand dollars to give. In any event, you may reach a point one day where your giving plan needs to become more sophisticated to accomplish all of your objectives. While you'll probably want to talk with a qualified financial advisor, it is helpful to have a basic understanding of the tools and techniques commonly used in the world of charitable "planned giving."

The major techniques fall into three broad categories: outright gifts, family foundations, and partial gifts. Keep in mind there are dozens of sophisticated techniques that can be creatively employed to achieve the best results for your situation, so consider this a primer, not an exhaustive list. Also, be aware that most large ministries and even some churches have staff members who focus on helping donors understand planned giving opportunities. Help is available if you need it.

Outright Gifts. As the name implies, you make these investments in your giving portfolio with no strings attached and nothing held back. Think of writing a check to your church or donating stock to a nonprofit organization. The majority of all gifts made to charities are outright gifts of money or property. From a financial standpoint, the donor is entitled to an income-tax deduction typically equal to the value of the gift.

EXAMPLES: OUTRIGHT GIFTS

Cash: Simplest and most time-efficient way to give, especially for smaller amounts.

Stock: Gifts of appreciated stock (public traded) have the added bonus of eliminating any gains in the stock without paying capital gains tax. Very good from a tax standpoint. Must have held the stock for at least a year to take advantage of this benefit. Check with the charity well ahead of time to make sure it has a brokerage account and can receive the stock.

Real Estate: Can be the gift of property or a qualified conservation easement (setting aside land for conservation purposes). Make sure the charity will accept the property before going too far down this road. Real estate can involve some tricky issues that some charities do not have the staff or inclination to deal with.

Family Foundations. Some time ago, one of my clients was experiencing the best year, financially, of his life. He had exercised some company stock options, and he was facing the mixed blessing of a huge income and a huge tax bill. He and his wife wanted to be able to invest a significant amount in their Eternity Portfolio but had no idea when or where. They also wanted to be able to include their children in the giving decisions over time. December 31 was fast approaching, so whatever they were going to do had to happen quickly. They decided to establish a private foundation.

The examples listed in the box on 202 are variations on what can loosely be called the "family foundation." They are ways to receive a current income-tax deduction while delaying the actual monetary transfer to the qualified charities.

Consider the example of the Fleming family (Case Study 3). Todd and Emily have just sold Industrial Solutions, Inc., and in addition to $3 million in outright gifts to different organizations, they have funded their private foundation with $2 million.

The Flemings receive an immediate income-tax deduction of $2 million. Their private foundation can distribute funds to any qualified charity that they as directors choose. There is no limit to how long the foundation can exist. Because it is a private foundation under current tax law, the Fleming Family Foundation must distribute at least 5 percent of its assets each year.

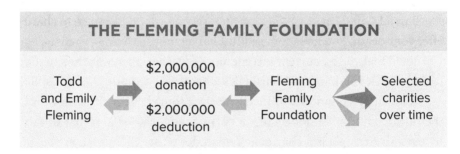

THE FLEMING FAMILY FOUNDATION

Todd and Emily Fleming → $2,000,000 donation → Fleming Family Foundation → Selected charities over time
$2,000,000 deduction

In family foundations the assets are transferred to an intermediate vehicle (see examples below) and then given to the designated charities at some later point. This can be a convenient tool for managing your Eternity Portfolio objectives in light of your income-tax situation. Family foundations can also be great teaching tools, allowing family members to be involved in the giving process at a higher level. Donor-advised funds are the most popular and convenient way to set up something that operates similar to a family foundation. They are provided by organizations such as the National Christian Foundation (see Appendix D) and are extremely efficient and convenient for making gifts.

EXAMPLES: FAMILY FOUNDATIONS

Donor-Advised Fund: A giving fund established at a brokerage firm, local community (or Christian community) foundation, or through an organization like the National Christian Foundation (www.nationalchristian.org). Also, check with your particular denomination to see if a foundation is available. Very little administration; no annual tax return filings. Most convenient way to set up a family foundation.

Private Foundation: Most flexible in terms of programs, operation, and control. However, also requires a good deal of administration in the areas of legal, accounting, and investments.

Supporting Organization: Typically established to support a particular charity. Allows the donor flexibility on timing and amount of eventual contributions to the supported organization.

Partial Gifts. Let's say you have an asset you would like to go to charity after your death. You need some additional income for living expenses, and you could really use a current income-tax deduction. Such was the situation faced by Rick and Barbara Cohen (Case Study 5).

With a partial gift, the ministry receives some benefit either now or in the future, and the donor retains a part of the asset for personal or family use. An example is a charitable remainder trust (CRT) such as the one the Cohens established. A CRT allows the donor to make a contribution of some amount in the future while receiving a current income-tax deduction *and keeping the income from the asset.*

The Cohens contributed $2 million to their CRT and "retained" an income interest of 5 percent. Until they both are deceased, they will receive 5 percent of the trust's value each year as an income stream. The first year that would be roughly $100,000. Whatever is left in the trust after their deaths will go to the charity. Based on their life expectancies, the current value of what the designated charity will eventually receive (as calculated using IRS tables) is $519,000. This is an estimate, but it is also the amount of tax deduction the IRS says the Cohens can claim for making the contribution. Since they retained a lifetime income from the trust, the charitable deduction is equal to the present value of the remainder interest. The charity only receives whatever *remains* after their deaths. (Note that the remainder interest calculation for tax purposes is dependent on tax law at the time of the gift. Another reason to seek competent tax counsel when considering any advanced strategies.)

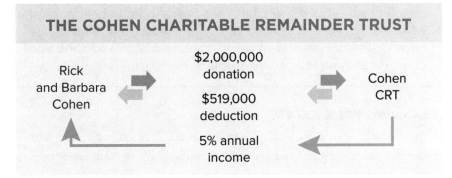

THE COHEN CHARITABLE REMAINDER TRUST

Rick and Barbara Cohen — $2,000,000 donation / $519,000 deduction / 5% annual income — Cohen CRT

There are quite a few variations on the CRT. Remember that typically the trust itself does not pay income tax. Instead, the donors pay taxes as the trust distributes the income. This makes the CRT particularly attractive if the donated asset carries a substantial capital gain. In effect, the tax is deferred for what could be decades while the assets inside the trust continue to grow. The Cohens can decide which charity (or charities) will receive the remainder interest and can design the trust with the flexibility to change the charitable beneficiary.

EXAMPLES: PARTIAL GIFTS

Charitable Remainder Trust: Donor contributes an asset and retains an income stream for life or a specific period up to twenty years. Current tax deduction is based on the present value of what the charity will eventually receive. Very effective for maximizing income-tax deduction on appreciated assets in one's estate that are planned for charity.

Charitable Gift Annuity: Donor makes a contribution directly to a charity in exchange for an annuity contract (the charity promises to pay the donor a set amount annually for life, or a certain period of years). Easier to establish and maintain than a CRT. Feasible for smaller contributions.

Charitable Lead Trust: The opposite of a CRT. Donor establishes a trust that provides an income stream to the charity for a fixed period of time. The donor's heirs are typically the beneficiaries of whatever remains at the end of the term. Used more for estate planning than income-tax planning because it decreases the value of the estate, and thus estate taxes.

PLANNING YOUR ESTATE

A great deal of charitable giving occurs at death. That probably makes sense under our old paradigm. Until you start thinking of giving as *investing* in your Eternity Portfolio, why would you make significant donations while there is any possibility you might still want the money for yourself? In fact, without the estate tax the question might become "Why would I *ever* make significant donations when there is the possibility that somebody in my family might need the money?"

I am convinced we should prayerfully reconsider any investment we could currently make in the Eternity Portfolio that is being delayed until our death. Think for a moment about two snowballs rolling downhill. If snowball A starts one thousand feet up the mountain and snowball B starts ten feet up the mountain, which snowball will be bigger at the bottom? The one that started higher up the mountain, of course.

When I say we should be hesitant to delay funding our Eternity Portfolio, I am thinking about compounding—what Einstein called the eighth great wonder of the world. When did you start saving for retirement? Maybe you're thinking, "I wish I'd started twenty years earlier than I did." The sooner you start, the longer the rewards compound. What about leverage for the kingdom? Suppose you had a plan to pass along a message to as many people as you possibly could in your lifetime. Everyone you talked to would give the message to five of their acquaintances, who would do the same with five of their acquaintances, and so on. How many more people would you reach if you started at age forty-five as opposed to age sixty-five? At sixty-five instead of eighty-five? Done properly, your investments should create an ever-expanding multiplier effect.

God is not calling everyone to give more immediately. There are two major exceptions to my premise about prayerfully reconsidering any delayed investment in the Eternity Portfolio. First is the inheritance to be passed along to your children. Obviously that would not be invested directly in your Eternity Portfolio. The second exception is what I would call your critical capital—the money you need to cover your living expenses (see chapter 5).

I realize that some people are led to give away everything they own and trust God literally to bring food and shelter to them on a daily basis. For many, however, our critical capital can be thought of as the farmland that provides our daily bread as God gives the increase. We certainly invest some of the "crop" in our Eternity Portfolio, and at some point God might call us to invest some or all of the land. Be willing, but be cautious. There aren't many examples in Scripture of people giving away all of their land.

Even if you have money set aside in these categories during your lifetime, you will still need to do some estate planning for the amount likely remaining when you die. That is where many of the techniques discussed earlier can be used effectively.

One final word of caution on setting up legacy gifts to charity: Even with the best planning, it is almost impossible to feel confident that a charitable entity you established at your death will still be following your wishes in even ten years, much less fifty. As Mark Twain once said, "Do your giving while you're living, so you're knowing where it's going."

YOUR LEGACY, YOUR CHOICE

You have been empowered to make a difference. The questions are, "How much?" and "For how long?" Be intentional about the process. Create a living legacy and a financial legacy to make an eternal difference for the kingdom of God. The coming generations will thank you.

ADVICE TO ADVISORS

For more than two decades now, God has allowed me the great privilege and responsibility to serve as an advisor. Across financial, investment, business, and life issues, I've had a front-row seat to the decision-making process of leaders and families, both wealthy and poor. Many reading this book share the high calling and responsibility of continuous learning and seeking God's face so they can provide wise counsel to others. When it comes to planning financial finish lines, investing in eternity, and leaving a legacy, the stakes are high. Your advice is a crucial component. Because the stakes are so high, particularly when it comes to giving away assets, we must, must, must avoid the big stumbling blocks that seem to trip up the unwary, the careless, and the inexperienced advisor. In addition to the basic idea that an advisor must never be satisfied with current levels of knowledge but always be growing, these are the big stumbling blocks to avoid:

1. Oversimplification. Too often advisors put too much emphasis on rules of thumb or even cookie-cutter solutions that don't allow for the freedom of the Holy Spirit or the unique experience of faith He may want for an individual. You shouldn't ignore conventional wisdom—often it has stood the test of time—but you should be willing to carefully test assumptions.

2. Getting caught up in the enthusiasm. The "spiritualness" of an idea or excitement over a new adventure makes people want to jump in. As a friend, we often want to cheer and encourage people to "just go for it." Advisors, however, must bring an encouraging but sober and insightful perspective.

3. Misunderstanding the interaction of faith and wisdom. Often people believe that faith and wisdom are opposites, but as Dallas Willard has said, "Faith is not opposed to knowledge, it is opposed to sight." Godly wisdom encompasses what has been discovered and is yet to be discovered by humans as wise and true at a natural level *and* then also includes elements that are only reachable at a supernatural level—true faith, hope, joy, forgiveness, and love.

4. Overspiritualizing. *Proper faith is not a leap in the dark.* If it were, the Scripture that says, "Faith comes by hearing" would be meaningless. Too many people make decisions as if God is going to constantly change His natural laws for them. My standard counsel to ministry leaders has become "Be careful how many miracles you need in your business plan." God created the world to work a certain way, and He seldom bends those natural laws. You may have to be the unpopular person who reminds investors of this. Do not allow yourself to be called unspiritual because you insist that someone consider genuine wisdom— whether financial, legal, or relational.

5. Missing the power of prayer. As strange as it sounds to our secularized ears, God really does respond to our prayers for wisdom and specific guidance. Make this a regular part of your daily disciplines to empower your advice.

6. Not leaning against conflicts of interest. Particularly in the financial services industry, make a practice of thinking about your conflicts of interest and asking, "Where should I proactively lean against my own interests to give proper advice?" When I was president of a wealth advisory firm, this became easier through the years. For instance, advising people to set aside cash from their portfolios when markets were expensive or encouraging them to give

Continued on next page

substantial amounts to charity. Both reduced my income, but I trusted that God would provide if I gave advice with integrity. As a direct consequence, my clients placed unwavering faith in my recommendations. They saw that I regularly put their interests ahead of my own.

7. Impatience. George MacDonald once wrote, "Impatience is a young man's vice." A wise friend once told me, "Let time be on your side." This is simple but powerful advice. Whenever possible, you should not allow yourself to be forced into snap judgments or quick advice. Insist on taking the time to think things through, pray, and let the process develop.

8. Advising on a road not traveled. As a young advisor, especially, you have to be careful not to overstep your experience. It's not that you can't advise on things you've never done, but there is a way to clearly spell out the best wisdom you have learned from study and application without being overly dogmatic about the best path for someone else. Part of your growth process, however, is to be moving down a path where you can apply that wisdom to your personal life. The goal is that eventually you have experience that can inform your advice at a deeper level. For instance, with generosity, if you're not in the game yourself, you shouldn't be pressuring others to give generously. Or, if you've never sold a business you spent thirty years building, be careful what you tell others they should do in that circumstance. Someone once told me when I was younger, "Everything's easy from the cheap seats with hotdog in hand." There is a lot of truth there. It's only when you've faced the personal, financial, and emotional pressures yourself that you can truly understand a client's decision making.

Once I had a business owner client who had just sold his company and believed God was calling him to use most of the proceeds—tens of millions of dollars—to start a ministry, to the point that he and his wife would have to start over financially if things didn't go well. As their advisor with concern for their financial well-being (not to mention fiduciary and legal responsibilities), this decision process stretched my faith and prayer life to new limits. Over the months as we worked on the project, I continuously asked this couple to tell me the specific things God was showing them—answers to prayer, specific direct guidance. They even had several prophetic dreams related to property purchases that came true! Without quenching the faith element, I felt strongly that it was my job to test and prod and make sure this couple wasn't kidding themselves that God was speaking—and further, what God was saying. We quantified how much is enough, which allowed them to see clearly how they would have to start over if certain things didn't work out. Finally, we structured the various parts of the transaction in as wise a fashion as possible with as many protections for their personal financial situation as we could.

The postscript is that the work of their ministry has gone extremely well and shows strong evidence of God's favor. At the same time, there has been strain on their personal financial situation that has brought about some of our worst-case scenarios. Even in that, God has a plan. They feel incredibly blessed to be about God's business and see His work firsthand.

As an advisor, you have an incredible responsibility. It should keep you prayerful, humble, and teachable. But people need your godly advice for the simple reason that their personal situation is usually the only one they have to work on. You've been given a valuable vantage point across many different situations that brings sorely needed perspective to those who want to live wisely.

DISCUSSION QUESTIONS

1. Have you considered what sort of "giving legacy" you would like to leave behind? What would you want your family and friends to say about your life when it is over?

2. If you knew you had ten years left to live, what would you do to create the sort of legacy you described above?

3. What financial lessons are you teaching your children? Is this happening intentionally or by accident?

4. When you consider the financial legacy you might leave, how much do you think is enough to empower your heirs without hindering their lives?

5. Once you have decided on your children's inheritance, what will you do with the rest of your estate? What might be the best ways for you to invest more in your Eternity Portfolio?

6. What do you think about the idea that we should prayerfully reconsider any investment we could currently make in the Eternity Portfolio that is being delayed until our death? How might this idea change your estate planning?

The Seven Golden Keys to Investing for Eternity

- ■ Honoring God
- ■ Creating maximum leverage through your giving

nvesting is more art than science. There is no one "best way" to achieve the desired results. However, though there are many methods for successful investing, a few guiding principles will take you a long way toward success no matter what the details. Concepts like proactive planning, diversification, long-term time horizon, and other boundary markers keep you on course to reach the goal.

In much the same way, there are keys to success when you're investing for eternity. Each key unlocks a part of God's heart and strategy for your Eternity Portfolio. Use the keys as a road map to direct your steps through much prayer and study of Scripture. Use them as an anvil on which to crush improper motives, beliefs, and actions. Use them as a window through which you see more clearly God's plan for the world and your part in it. Use the keys to unleash the incredible joy that comes from the integration of your whole being—time, talents, and treasure—into God's unique purpose for you.

◆━ THE CONVICTION PRINCIPLE

Conviction dictates action. What you believe about investing determines how you invest, how much you invest, and how long you invest. Conviction starts with understanding truth and progresses to the logical implications of that truth. It's the "values transformed to vision" formula from chapter 1.

The Eternity Portfolio is one of those progressions. It is the logical extension of biblical truth as applied to our financial resources. But *to make the jump from mere knowledge to a vision that generates results, you have to truly believe.* Let's look at three convictions that are central to the Eternity Portfolio concept:

- **Relationship.** Everything in the Christian life begins with a personal relationship with God through Jesus Christ. God Himself draws us into relationship by giving us the power to believe the truth presented in the Bible. Through repentance of our sins and faith in Christ we become His children and heirs of all the promises of Scripture. *Conviction about our relationship with God is the foundation on which we base our actions.*

- **Response.** A personal relationship with God brings the conviction that we need to respond to God's love. We are empowered by the Holy Spirit to love Him and learn through the Bible what that means. Part of this conviction is that God has a plan for our lives that we can discover by studying Scripture, and we need to be in alignment with that plan. Jesus referred to this plan when He said, "If you keep My commandments, you will abide in My love" (John 15:10). The apostle John wrote strong words about those who want to say they know God but do not follow in His path: "Now by this we know that we know Him, if we keep His commandments. He who says, 'I know Him,' and does not keep His commandments, is a liar, and the truth is not in him" (1 John 2:3–4). *The faithful manager holds the strong conviction that God has given us timeless truths in the Bible and those truths form the foundation for how he or she should live.*

- **Rewards.** God has used the prospect of eternal rewards as a motivator throughout His recorded dealings with humankind. *The faithful manager is convinced that God will not forget his or her labors on this earth.* Scripture encourages this conviction: "But without faith it is impossible to please Him, for he who comes to God must believe that He is, and that He is a *rewarder* of those who diligently seek Him" (Hebrews 11:6, emphasis added). God rewards our faith in Him with eternal life, and He rewards the evidence of that faith through the work of our lives with eternal rewards. He devised the plan, and it is only by His grace that we have this prospect.

Nowhere is the progression from relationship to response to rewards demonstrated more succinctly than in two short verses describing the life of Moses.

> By faith Moses, when he became of age, refused to be called the son of Pharaoh's daughter, choosing rather to suffer affliction with the people of God than to enjoy the passing pleasures of sin, esteeming the reproach of Christ greater riches than the treasures in Egypt; for he looked to the reward. (Hebrews 11:24–26)

Moses believed God and chose to live in light of that conviction in pursuit of the reward. You have to believe to catch the vision of the Eternity Portfolio as the ultimate long-term investment for your money. Faith, and thereby conviction, is a progression. As you grow in understanding God's Word, your faith grows. And true faith always proves itself through action.

The entire book of James speaks to the fact that faith must bear fruit. As you ponder the conviction principle, think about convictions that flow out of a proper perspective on investing in eternity. How does the Eternity Portfolio affect your outlook on work? On family? On greed? On priorities?

◆— THE COMMUNION PRINCIPLE

God is infinitely creative in His dealings with people. The Christian life is not about rules, formulas, and rigid structure. Just about the time you think you have His plan all figured out, He moves in another direction—always accomplishing His plan from before the foundation of the world but in a different way from any you've observed before.

Although God gave us incredible wisdom in the Bible, He purposely did not fill in all the blanks. We must apply many of the principles we understand in ways not specified in Scripture. We end up scratching our heads as we see God working out the *application* in vastly different ways around the world. *How am I specifically to carry out His will? Should I go about it this way or that? Either way could be effective. How do I choose?*

When it comes to investing for eternity, the questions are just as complicated. Why does God call some people to give away all of their money while others are perfectly within His will when they give only a portion? Is it possible He exercises the faith of one woman in *giving away* the family business while directing another to *build* a business that generates funds for the kingdom? What amount should I give systematically? How does one know when to give spontaneously over and above a systematic plan? All of these questions require specific revelation of God's will in our lives. How do we get that?

The communion principle is the understanding that without ongoing, regular time spent communing with God, we cannot know His specific will for our lives. This communion starts with regular, disciplined time alone in prayer and Bible study, but it is so much more than that. It is the state of abiding in God's presence, being quiet before Him, and listening for His direction. Sometimes He gives that direction explicitly through Scripture or the godly teaching and counsel of others. However, many times it comes from the quiet voice of the Holy Spirit that guides us in the proper direction. Communion is a day-by-day and hour-by-hour activity that becomes your life over time. God desires fellowship with you, and the revelation of His plan for you depends on it.

> In my daily fellowship with the Lord in His Word I sense Him speaking to me about my giving. Often He lays someone on my heart that begins with prayer for them, fellowship later, and support eventually.
>
> *Dr. Johnny Hunt*

Ongoing communion with God affects three specific areas of your Eternity Portfolio. First, godly **motives** will stay at the forefront of your giving. In the words of Bill Bright:

> Godly motives stem from a cheerful, loving heart for God. We give to please our Lord and express our love to Him. We give out of obedience to our Lord's command to lay up treasures in heaven. We give to be a channel of God's abundant resources to a desperately needy world. We give to help fulfill the Great Commission and thus help reach the world for Christ.[1]

Second, He will guide you regarding the **means** of your giving. In carrying out His plan for your life, God knows exactly how much you are to invest in your Eternity Portfolio, and He will show you over time. Finally, as you commune with God, He will make the **methods** of proper giving clear. This is the "when and how" part of the equation. He will guide your planned and spontaneous giving to be most effective.

Do not fall into the trap of assuming that what God has led you to do will remain static over time. Part of the faith journey is that we don't know what the future holds. God does. Only through continual communion with Him will you be most effective in your giving.

◆━☞ THE CONDUCTION PRINCIPLE

When you turn on the water faucet in your house, what happens? If everything operates properly and you have paid the water bill, water streams forth in a seemingly endless supply. But what was necessary for that simple end result to occur? In most cases in North America, there was an elaborate plan to transport the water from a river, stream, or lake through miles of pipeline into your house. Along the way, countless pumping and filtration systems conduct that water in usable form to its final destination. Tens of thousands of people spend their working lives planning, executing, and evaluating this process to further the vision of clean, usable water delivered to every home.

Vision leads to strategy. Just as God gives you the vision for your Eternity Portfolio, He will also lead you to the proper strategy for executing the plan. Your job is to be intentional about the plan and to use your God-given wisdom and intelligence to flesh out the details. Don't be confused into thinking that planning is unspiritual or shows a lack of trust in God. On the contrary, God ordained planning. Think of how He has worked throughout history. God gave Noah a one-hundred-year plan for building the ark. God gave the Israelites a detailed plan for worshiping Him. Solomon executed a plan to build the temple. On and on the story goes. God has used short-term and long-term plans to accomplish His purposes through those who would listen and obey. The key is that they received His plan and were sensitive to His leading throughout the process of completing it. We must maintain a balance and make sure we don't override God's plan with our own "wisdom."

God is the main reservoir of all material riches. *The conduction principle is God's big plan for giving: to channel those resources through faithful managers to others.* He has millions of "faucets" around the world where people need the "water." Your position is to be a conduit or pipeline.

We see this concept throughout the Bible: "Give, and it will be given to you: good measure, pressed down, shaken together, and running over will be put into your bosom. For with the same measure that you use, it will be measured back to you" (Luke 6:38).

You are blessed to be a blessing. As a conduit, the faithful manager is careful to seek out God's will as to the volume (how much), the timing (when), and the direction (where) of the flow of resources.

> I often have to ask, *"Lord, who did you give me this gift for?"* It is often so clear that what I possess is not for me. Remember, it's not about me. I must constantly remind myself of this truth.
>
> *Dr. Johnny Hunt*

> After fifteen years of spending time with wealthy people across the globe, the most godly and happy people I know are the most generous. Their whole orientation is to be a blessing to others.
>
> *Todd Harper*

THE COMBUSTION PRINCIPLE

As you evaluate specific investments for your Eternity Portfolio, think about the 80/20 rule: on average, for any given endeavor, 20 percent of the energy will cause 80 percent of the impact. You can apply this concept to almost any activity. Within churches, the vast majority of the funding (80 percent or more) comes from a small percentage of the families in attendance. In business, most of the productivity comes from 20 percent or less of the employees.

This rule applies to your giving. Look for ministry opportunities where one little spark can lead to an explosion of results. Think of starting a massive avalanche with one little rock. You must, however, push the rock from a strategic high place where exactly the right conditions exist to create a disproportionately large result. Your Eternity Portfolio investment is the little rock.

Looking for combustion opportunities is like looking for investment opportunities early in their life cycle. It is at that point that, if correctly identified, the opportunity will generate the highest long-term return with the smallest initial investment.

> One family I know liked the idea of making some riskier investments but didn't want their whole Eternity Portfolio spent that way, so they decided on a certain percentage they would invest each year in "not sure things." The factor that distinguished whether they would make a riskier investment was whether they thought the upside of that success would be ten times their investment. So they were willing to take risk, but only if it might have incredible leverage.
>
> *Heather Tuininga*

> I think about "derivative works" as described by Jesus in Matthew 25:34-40. These are ways we don't even contemplate or comprehend that God is using us to create His result. We won't know, maybe ever, the full extent of our impact.
>
> *Jack Alexander*

The combustion principle means that you look for investments that result in exponential (as opposed to incremental) growth for the kingdom of God. One example would be a church-planting movement that is sweeping across a continent or country. Another would be a discipleship strategy for training and equipping pastors. Think again of the ripples created in that pond when you toss in a pebble. You have the option to invest in one person throwing pebbles or one person recruiting and training other people to throw pebbles. Which will have the most compounding impact over time?

COMBUSTION OPPORTUNITIES ARE OFTEN BEYOND THE FRONT LINES

While many want to be "on the front lines" where they can experience some immediate impact of helping, the root causes (particularly in poverty and social justice) tend to be solved behind the scenes and over longer periods of time. It is tedious, messy, and anything but an emotional rush. However, when you work at the roots of a problem the impact of momentum toward a solution is huge. As Martin Luther King Jr., said, "Philanthropy is commendable, but it must not cause the philanthropist to overlook the circumstances . . . which make philanthropy necessary." *Solving root causes are combustion opportunities of the highest order.*

Look for fields that are "white for harvest" (John 4:35), and invest there. You will also have investments that are exploratory, and you will almost certainly occasionally dig some dry wells. However, when it is obvious that God is working in a certain space or time, make sure you concentrate major dollars there. *Focus on opportunities that have the potential to explode for the kingdom.*

THE COMPASSION PRINCIPLE

"But whoever has this world's goods, and sees his brother in need, and shuts up his heart from him, how does the love of God abide in him?" (1 John 3:17). When God designed the world and the people who would inhabit it, He could have set things up so there would be no needs. No need for food. No need for clothing. No need for shelter. But for whatever reason, He allowed the system to operate so that, according to the words of Jesus, the poor would always be with us.

The compassion principle is this: Our response to the needs of the poor reflects our heart for God. If we really love Him, that love cannot help but show itself in love for others. How would the world look differently at the Christian community in the twenty-first century if we invested our resources where we say our values lie? Roman emperors were once motivated to set up hospitals and other institutions to care for the sick and widows and orphans because of the Christian service around them. It wasn't so much that the Romans were concerned about the care of needy people but that they did not want the Christians alone to have such a noble reputation! Apparently the praise of the Christians was reaching jealous ears. Perhaps this is what Jesus was talking about when He said, "Let your light so shine before men, that they may see your good works and glorify your Father in heaven" (Matthew 5:16).

Is your compassion level where you want it? Are you actively aware of opportunities to invest in providing for the base-level needs of hurting people? The rest of the world is watching to see whether modern Christians really *will* help. I am convinced that when we love people at every level of society, meeting their needs from a heart of compassion and genuine concern, God uses that to show Himself to the world. You want to be a part of this.

THE CONNECTION PRINCIPLE

The intersection of your personal life mission with your giving—and then with others—is one of the most powerful combinations you will ever experience. As you connect through your Eternity Portfolio strategy, relationships flourish between other givers, leaders, and ministry co-workers not only resulting in creative, innovative, and expanding results for the kingdom, but also expanding your personal joy through working in community. My deepest relationships are those I've built through a shared love of investing in God's kingdom together. What a blessing of connection!

Then, I can't emphasize enough the need to connect your calling with your Eternity Portfolio. Through the process you will move beyond merely funding the work of the kingdom to the actual ministry work itself. Many times organizations need your wisdom, your time, and especially your prayers as much as your money.

Where your treasure is, there your heart will be also (see Matthew 6:21)—although it is not always easy to determine which comes first in that equation. We are certainly more interested in something after we invest in it. (You probably never followed a particular company's stock price until you bought some shares, for example.) However, I also believe that if the heart pulls in a given direction, the money eventually follows. This is consistent with research by the Gallup organization.

> We discovered that often people donate time and energy first, then make serious financial commitments to the church later. Why? Because after becoming an active part of the faith community and its ministry, people not only have a vested interest in funding the work, but also truly own the ministry . . . a powerful link between giving money and giving time to a church.[2]

Pursue this connection and take advantage of the opportunities to get involved in ministry at a deeper level. You'll have a much better understanding of whether the organization is one you should continue supporting.

Finally, the connection principle relates to connecting your children to the process of giving, which we've already discussed in detail in chapter 8. Remember to bring them in early and reinforce the connection regularly over time. Your legacy to future generations will be evidence of the connection you achieved with your own family.

> What are you doing to spread the message of generosity itself? No matter how generous you are, there will likely be a whole lot more created for God's kingdom if you use your influence in addition to your affluence.
>
> *Larry Powell*

THE CONSECRATION PRINCIPLE

There is a videotaped interview of Bill and Vonette Bright I've watched a number of times because it shines so brightly as an example of the consecration principle. In the Brights' more than fifty years of ministry, they may have impacted more people for the cause of Christ than anyone in modern history. Through Campus Crusade for Christ (now CRU), the ministry Dr. Bright founded in 1952, millions of people around the world have been touched with the love of Christ. And thousands of churches and ministries have been birthed by people formerly connected with CRU.

In the interview, Dr. Bright spoke about the "contract" he and Vonette, his wife, made with God more than fifty years earlier. When Bill left a job in business to follow God's call, they committed everything to Him. As they lived on a modest salary, never accepting honorariums or book royalties, God directed hundreds of millions of dollars through them to His kingdom purposes. God always abundantly met their needs. Vonette says that God has not been "shabby" in allowing them to enjoy many things in this life.

There was a glow on the Brights' faces as they talked about God as a close friend. They talked about how He had brought them along this marvelous journey and allowed them to be a part of His plan. Bill's health had declined, and he was wearing an oxygen tube during the interview. But there was still an aura that seemed to emanate from the couple. Then I realized what it was: I was watching the *overflow of a life fully consecrated to God*.

The consecration principle is this convergence of our life into the image of Christ. It is evident when we begin to understand that *everything is given over to Him* and no earthly things are really that important when compared to the joy of knowing Him.

We move through a progression in our giving. What often begins as an obligation moves to an opportunity and then eventually to a pure overflow of the generous life. Along the way our motivations change. The continuum

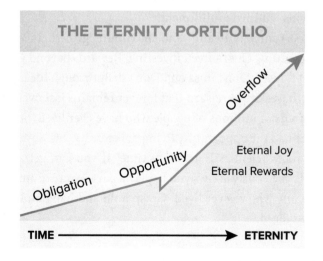

THE ETERNITY PORTFOLIO

Overflow

Opportunity

Obligation

Eternal Joy
Eternal Rewards

TIME ⟶ ETERNITY

might look something like this chart. What starts as obedience gives way to a gratitude that brings a more willing offering. Next we develop an increased vision about the opportunity for eternal rewards. Finally our experience of giving and our sense of God's presence in our life manifest themselves in a joy that is not only visible but contagious. The generous life overflows.

I *believe* this is how it works. In all honesty, I'm not there yet. I see glimpses of the overflow at times, and I see evidence of it in other people who are further along in the journey. To glorify God is our chief aim, and His glory radiates from those who have fully consecrated their lives to Him. Take notice of others who seem to be moving in this direction. Ask them their story. Ask about their attitude on giving. My guess is that they have extremely generous hearts. Your Eternity Portfolio can be the start or the acceleration of this transformation in your own life.

THE ULTIMATE INVESTMENT OPPORTUNITY

I have worked with wealthy investors for years; God has allowed me personally to manage more money than most people will ever see. Through personal and professional experience I've observed that although money can be a great tool, it *never* determines the level of joy or satisfaction in a person's life. Used properly, money can facilitate some great experiences. Used improperly, it can be devastating. But true joy and happiness are there for the taking no matter whether you have much money or little. The proper alignment of God's purpose in your life with your relationships and your resources brings ultimate fulfillment.

The opportunity is before you: maximum growth investing. Really long-term investing. Guaranteed investing. Rewards beyond your imagination that last forever. Don't miss out. Don't drift through life laying up treasures on earth, seeking a reward that forever remains just over the horizon. Of the hundreds of millions of people who have ever lived, only a precious few have ever had the opportunity to impact eternity this way. The kingdom of God advances relentlessly through time! If you can get a piece of the action—if He graciously allows you to play a part—you are among the most fortunate of any who've ever lived. Grasp hold and hang on tightly to that which is life indeed.

Do not lay up for yourselves treasures on earth, where moth and rust destroy and where thieves break in and steal; but lay up for yourselves treasures in heaven, where neither moth nor rust destroys and where thieves do not break in and steal. For where your treasure is, there your heart will be also. (Matthew 6:19–21)

DISCUSSION QUESTIONS

1. Which of the seven principles (conviction, communion, conduction, combustion, compassion, connection, consecration) is the most challenging for you? Why?

2. What do you think of the idea that the intersection of your personal life mission with your giving is an unusually powerful combination (the connection principle)? How are you developing a stronger sense of your personal mission?

3. What changes might you make in your Eternity Portfolio as a result of these principles?

APPENDIX A
Case Studies

ABOUT THE CASE STUDIES

These fictitious examples show how five families set about developing and implementing their Eternity Portfolio strategies. (Special thank you to Charlie Jordan for his help editing and reviewing the case studies!) Though they are from different backgrounds, family situations, and income levels, they share a pursuit of the ultimate investment.

The numbers representing each family's financial situation are not meant to be exact. The nature of financial projections is that they are merely a "best guess" based on hypothetical growth rates, taxes, and earnings. The investing strategies used by each family are representative of the variety of ways people can go about creating an Eternity Portfolio. None is to be considered the *best* way for you and your family; these are merely ideas to be explored through prayer and God's leading in your own life.

Case Study 1: Donna Rutherford—single, no children, annual income of $74,000

Case Study 2: John and Sheila Patterson—married, two children ages six and four, annual combined income of $58,000

Case Study 3: Todd and Emily Fleming—married, four children ages eight to fourteen, annual combined income varies but approximately $15 million this year due to sale of business

Case Study 4: Ben Richards—widowed, four children ages fifteen to twenty-eight, annual income of $28,000

Case Study 5: Rick and Barbara Cohen—married, one child age twenty-six, annual income ranges between $200,000 and $300,000 but due to stock-option exercise is approximately $5 million this year

> As you read these different scenarios of giving, something will probably happen in your heart: the question will arise, "How about me and my family? Where do we fit in the context of Kingdom generosity?" As you seriously seek the Lord on this question, believe me, the joy that follows an obedient life is the purest of joys!
>
> *Dr. Johnny Hunt*

DONNA RUTHERFORD—CASE 1

Born and raised in Minneapolis, Minnesota, Donna Rutherford has two driving passions. First, as a Christian since age twelve, Donna sees her personal relationship with God as the most important thing in her life. Second, she feels her life's mission is to be a part of global evangelism.

That's where her "real job" comes in. Just before her thirty-fifth birthday, Donna became the youngest regional vice president ever at United Package Company. Now forty-seven, she spends most of her time traveling around the world overseeing logistics at UPC's foreign operational branches. As God has developed Donna's understanding of His plan for her life, she has become a sought-after resource within the church because of her international network. Donna serves on the missions committee of her church and is on the board of an organization called Global Outreach for Asian Regions (GOFAR).

Although Donna hasn't given a great deal of thought to retiring, she uses age sixty-seven in her planning. Retirement seems like a long way off, but she is currently saving 15 percent of her annual income for that purpose. Once she turns fifty-six, Donna plans to decrease annual retirement savings to 12 percent. Her goal over the next several decades is to maintain her current standard of living (adjusted for inflation) while investing an increasing amount in her Eternity Portfolio. Donna sees her current plan as a baseline for discerning

ETERNITY PORTFOLIO
INVESTMENT SCHEDULE

INCOME	GIVING PERCENTAGE
$0-25,000	10 %
$25,001-50,000	15 %
$50,001-100,000	25 %
$100,001-150,000	30 %
$150,001-up	50 %

God's will in this area of her life. She is sensitive to the fact that God may lead her to invest larger amounts over and above her planned giving.

Over the next thirty years, Donna will invest almost $500,000 in her Eternity Portfolio based on the current projections. A comparison of her Family

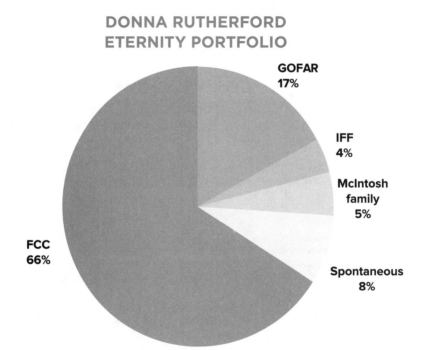

DONNA RUTHERFORD ETERNITY PORTFOLIO

GOFAR 17%

IFF 4%

McIntosh family 5%

Spontaneous 8%

FCC 66%

CURRENT YEAR ALLOCATION

LOCAL CHURCH

Fellowship Community Church	$8,000

PERSONAL MISSION

Global Outreach for Asian Regions	$2,100

POOR

International Famine Fund	$500
McIntosh family	$650

SPONTANEOUS

| | $1,000 |

| | TOTAL | **$12,250** |

Portfolio (mostly retirement assets) and her Eternity Portfolio over the years might look something like the graph below. Donna recognizes that, based on a

FINANCIAL PROJECTION — Donna Rutherford

	Today	10 years	20 years	30 years
Donna's age	47	57	67	77
CASH FLOW				
Income				
Donna - UPC	74,000	99,450	133,652	-
Retirement Plans	-	-	-	61,559
Other Investments	-	-	-	19,375
Total	**74,000**	**99,450**	**133,652**	**80,934**
Expenses				
Mtg & R.E. taxes	11,296	12,036	13,029	5,219
Income & Social Security taxes	14,467	21,004	30,580	12,312
General living	22,356	30,045	40,377	54,264
Investing				
Retirement Plans	11,100	11,934	16,038	-
Other Investments	2,531	5,819	4,782	-
Eternity Portfolio	12,250	18,612	28,846	9,140
Total	**74,000**	**99,450**	**133,652**	**80,934**
ASSETS				
Home	188,000	252,656	339,549	456,325
Mortgage	-132,429	-107,671	-64,813	-
Retirement Plans	193,321	510,480	1,097,315	1,321,785
Other Investments	14,300	74,497	216,226	28,391
Total Family Portfolio	**263,192**	**729,962**	**1,588,277**	**1,806,501**

conservative growth rate of 6 percent on the Family Portfolio, she might accumulate as much as $1.8 million over thirty years. Using our earlier analogy of 10,000 percent returns in the Eternity Portfolio, we can estimate the value of her investment there as well.

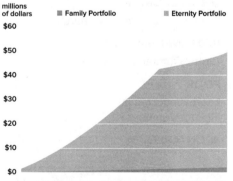

RUTHERFORD - 30 YEARS OF GROWTH

JOHN AND SHEILA PATTERSON—CASE 2

Several miles west of Jacksonville, Florida, is a small community called Middleburg, where John and Sheila Patterson have just purchased their first home. They have been married for almost ten years and have two children. The oldest, Shannon, is just finishing the first grade while Jason will be starting kindergarten next year. Sheila is a legal assistant at Baker & McCoy law offices. John is the youth pastor at Middleburg First Presbyterian Church. Both Sheila and John feel called to mentor young adults in their community, especially as they are involved at church.

When it comes to saving for the future, the Pattersons have a plan. They are diligent to invest 10 percent of their income toward retirement and intend to increase that to 15 percent at age forty-five and 20 percent at fifty-five. Each year they save 4 percent of their income for the children's college education. Although the college fund will probably not pay all the expenses for both Shannon and Jason, they hope to be able to help out with additional money when the time comes.

ETERNITY PORTFOLIO
INVESTMENT SCHEDULE

INCOME	GIVING PERCENTAGE
$0-40,000	10 %
$40,001-70,000	12 %
$70,001-100,000	18 %
$100,001-130,000	25 %
$130,001-170,000	35 %
$170,001-up	50 %

John and Sheila have served meals at a local homeless shelter with their children. They are excited about the possibility of investing financially in the shelter at some point in the future. Over their lifetime, the Pattersons hope to invest more than $1 million in the kingdom of God.

Even at such early ages, Shannon and Jason are starting to catch the vision too. They are already giving part of their allowance on a regular basis.

JOHN & SHEILA PATTERSON
ETERNITY PORTFOLIO

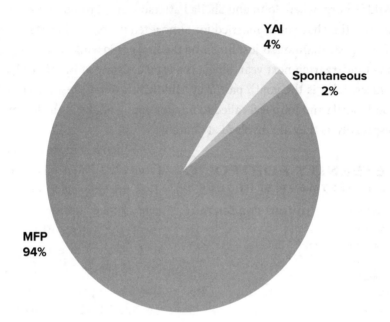

YAI
4%

Spontaneous
2%

MFP
94%

CURRENT YEAR ALLOCATION

LOCAL CHURCH
Middleburg First Presbyterian $5,800

PERSONAL MISSION
Youth Alive, Inc. $240

SPONTANEOUS $120

                                    TOTAL   **$6,160**

FINANCIAL PROJECTION John and Sheila Patterson

	Today	10 years	20 years	30 years
John's age	31	41	51	61
Sheila's age	32	42	52	62
CASH FLOW				
Income				
John	26,000	36,676	51,735	72,977
Sheila	32,000	45,139	63,673	89,817
Total	**58,000**	**81,815**	**115,408**	**162,794**
Expenses				
Mtg & R.E. taxes	10,243	10,983	11,976	5,219
Income & Social Security taxes	8,352	13,254	17,023	23,975
General living	24,961	33,545	45,082	60,587
Investing				
Retirement Plans	5,800	8,181	17,293	29,698
College Funding	2,320	3,273	-	-
Other Investments	164	2,852	7,181	11,338
Eternity Portfolio	6,160	9,727	16,852	31,978
Total	**58,000**	**81,815**	**115,407**	**162,795**
ASSETS				
Home	125,000	167,990	225,764	303,408
Mortgage	-117,181	-95,272	-57,347	-
Retirement Plans	5,800	101,692	354,333	965,490
Other Investments	164	28,780	124,936	301,618
College Funding	2,390	35,236	-	-
Total Family Portfolio	**16,173**	**238,426**	**647,686**	**1,570,516**

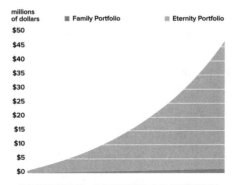

PATTERSON - 30 YEARS OF GROWTH

TODD AND EMILY FLEMING—CASE 3

In 1952, Todd's father began Industrial Solutions, Inc., a manufacturer of cleaning chemicals in suburban Dallas. Todd started in the business when he was sixteen and has played a key role in its growth and expansion over the past ten years, especially after his father passed away four years ago. Industrial Solutions was sold this year for $60 million, which was roughly twice the amount that the family had invested over the years. The proceeds were split evenly between Todd and his younger sister.

ETERNITY PORTFOLIO
INVESTMENT SCHEDULE

INCOME	GIVING PERCENTAGE
$0-40,000	10 %
$40,001-100,000	20 %
$100,001-200,000	30 %
$200,001-300,000	50 %
$300,001-up	70 %

Todd and his wife, Emily, have four children between the ages of eight and fourteen. In addition to running the business and raising a family, they are actively involved in fundraising for a Christian university in Dallas. Also, they are extremely concerned about the plight of women and children around the world, particularly those in poverty-stricken areas.

As he was selling the business, many well-meaning friends encouraged Todd to retire and go into some sort of vocational ministry. Todd, however, really felt God wanted him to start another business so he could continue to use his business platform to the glory of God. Also, Todd and Emily both believe that Todd is gifted as an entrepreneur and that a new business would be a major source of additional investments in the Eternity Portfolio. The Flemings anticipate several more substantial investments in their Eternity Portfolio over and above the annual contributions. One idea they are already considering is the contribution of all of the stock in Fleming Industries to the Fleming Family Foundation. The projections given in the chart reflect this happening at age sixty. Obviously, this assumes significant growth over the coming years. Emily has begun to make plans related to a crisis-pregnancy center idea for the Foundation. Todd and Emily plan to allow their children to join them on the foundation's distribution committee when they reach age sixteen.

TODD & EMILY FLEMING
ETERNITY PORTFOLIO

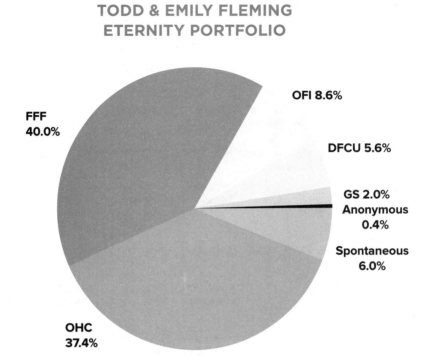

FFF 40.0%

OFI 8.6%

DFCU 5.6%

GS 2.0%
Anonymous 0.4%

Spontaneous 6.0%

OHC 37.4%

CURRENT YEAR ALLOCATION

LOCAL CHURCH

Oak Hills Church	$1,870,000

PERSONAL MISSION

Fleming Family Foundation	$2,000,000
Orphan Flight, Inc.	$430,000
DF Christian University	$280,000

POOR

Global Seed	$100,000
Anonymous gifts	$20,000

SPONTANEOUS	$300,000

	TOTAL	**$5,000,000**

FINANCIAL PROJECTION Todd and Emily Fleming

	Today	10 years	20 years	30 years
Todd's age	44	54	64	74
Emily's age	42	52	62	72

CASH FLOW
Income

Todd-Fleming Industries	325,000	842,966	-	-
Sale of Industrial Solutions, Inc.	30,000,000	-	-	-
Other investments	-	2,153,278	1,248,114	1,311,943
Total	**30,325,000**	**2,996,244**	**1,248,114**	**1,311,943**

Expenses

R.E. taxes	6,200	8,332	11,198	15,049
Income & Social Security taxes	2,065,000	521,426	214,501	224,323
General living	140,328	217,925	262,736	268,211

Investing

Fleming Industries	22,830,000	-	-	-
College Funding	275,000	-	-	-
Other Investments	-	265,189	-	-
Eternity Portfolio	5,000,000	1,983,371	759,680	804,360
Total	**30,316,528**	**2,996,243**	**1,248,115**	**1,311,943**

ASSETS

Home	470,000	631,641	848,872	1,140,813
Fleming Industries	22,830,000	59,215,140	-	-
Other investments	4,987,000	11,234,432	22,806,454	23,972,779
College Funding	275,000	169,052	-	-
Total Family Portfolio	**28,562,000**	**71,250,265**	**23,655,326**	**25,113,592**

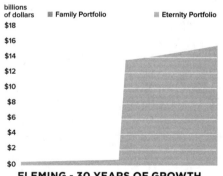

FLEMING - 30 YEARS OF GROWTH

BEN RICHARDS—CASE 4

Ben Richards lives in Westin, a small community outside of Buffalo, New York, with his son, Brad (age fifteen). His older daughters, Laura and Lisa, are both married, and his youngest daughter, Abby, is away at college in Connecticut. Now fifty-seven, Ben has worked for twenty-eight years at Municipal Electric Corporation. Although of modest means, he has been saving for retirement over the years and will also receive a nice pension at age sixty-five. Ben has helped each of his children with college, although they have also taken advantage of scholarships and work-study programs.

ETERNITY PORTFOLIO
INVESTMENT SCHEDULE

INCOME	GIVING PERCENTAGE
$0-20,000	10 %
$20,001-40,000	15 %
$40,001-80,000	20 %
$80,001-up	40 %

Ben has been active in several short-term missions efforts at his church where his skills as an electrician have been particularly useful. Most of these projects have been connected with Russian orphanages that were either under construction or in need of significant repairs. He is excited about the prospect of being able to contribute even more after retirement—both financially and with his time. Ben is also starting to see gratifying results from the years of training his children. Both Laura and Lisa have great families and are faithful managers of their family resources with their husbands, and Abby is involved in the college group at a church in Connecticut.

BEN RICHARDS
ETERNITY PORTFOLIO

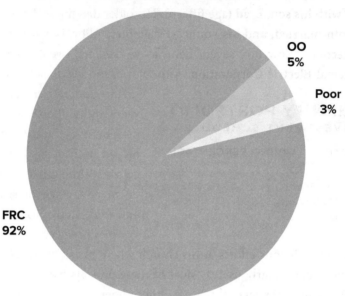

OO
5%

Poor
3%

FRC
92%

CURRENT YEAR ALLOCATION

LOCAL CHURCH
First Redeemer $2,950

PERSONAL MISSION
ORT Outreach $150

POOR $100

TOTAL **$3,200**

FINANCIAL PROJECTION   Ben Richards

	Today	10 years	20 years	30 years
Ben's age	57	67	77	87

CASH FLOW

Income

Ben-Municipal Electric	28,000	-	-	-
Pension and Social Security	-	28,304	34,502	42,058
Other investments	-	3,729	4,749	8,024
Total	**28,000**	**32,033**	**39,251**	**50,082**

Expenses

Mtg & R.E. taxes	2,770	2,959	993	1,335
Income & Social Security taxes	5,040	4,246	6,210	7,570
General living	16,990	21,023	27,160	34,160

Investing

Eternity Portfolio	3,200	3,805	4,888	7,016
Total	**28,000**	**32,033**	**39,251**	**50,081**

ASSETS

Home	82,000	110,201	148,101	199,036
Mortgage	-21,643	-7,956	-	-
Other investments	59,600	95,102	121,101	133,738
Total Family Portfolio	**119,957**	**197,347**	**269,202**	**332,774**

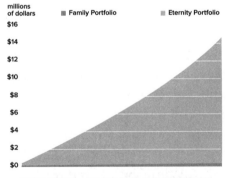

RICHARDS - 30 YEARS OF GROWTH

RICK AND BARBARA COHEN—CASE 5

Rick and Barbara Cohen have been investing for years. In addition to sizable retirement accounts, Rick has roughly $8 million in company stock options and Barbara owns one-half of Cohen & Braden, CPAs. Even though they have been investing in their Eternity Portfolio for some time, the Cohens feel that now is the time to really increase their giving. This year they will exercise and sell $5 million in stock options to start the process. Of that amount, they will use $2 million to fund a charitable remainder trust, they'll invest $1.7 million in their Eternity Portfolio, and the balance will go to pay income taxes. The Cohens plan to use the annual payments from the charitable remainder trust to fund a portion of their retirement income needs.

ETERNITY PORTFOLIO
INVESTMENT SCHEDULE

INCOME	GIVING PERCENTAGE
$0-100,000	10 %
$100,001-200,000	15 %
$200,001-300,000	20 %
$300,001-up	30 %

Rick has been involved in church-planting efforts for several years now and believes a significant portion of their portfolio should be devoted to this purpose. Barbara considers her gifts to be in the area of helping people become more faithful with their time, abilities, and resources. Her favorite investment, Christian Life Managers, empowers people to explore their God-given life purpose in order to make a difference for the kingdom of God. The Cohens also desire to make a major investment in homeless ministries focused in the San Francisco Bay area, where they live. They intend to accomplish this over the next few years using the money invested in their donor-advised fund, which was set up as part of their current year's Eternity Portfolio investment (see chart below).

Although Rick is "retiring" to be more involved in ministry, Barbara intends to work at her CPA firm for at least three more years. At that time, they are considering another major investment in the Eternity Portfolio.

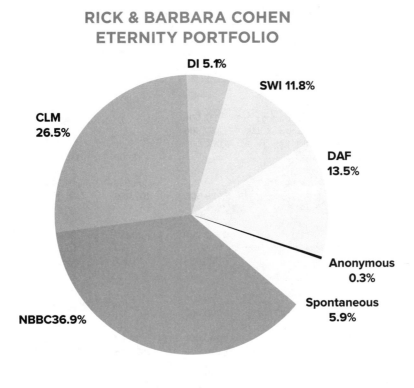

RICK & BARBARA COHEN ETERNITY PORTFOLIO

DI 5.1%

SWI 11.8%

CLM
26.5%

DAF
13.5%

Anonymous
0.3%

Spontaneous
5.9%

NBBC 36.9%

CURRENT YEAR ALLOCATION

LOCAL CHURCH

North Bay Baptist Church	$628,000

PERSONAL MISSION

Christian Life Managers	$450,000
Disciple International	$87,000
Simple Water, Inc.	$200,000

POOR

Donor-Advised Fund	$230,000
Anonymous gifts	$5,000

SPONTANEOUS | $100,000

TOTAL	**$1,700,000**

FINANCIAL PROJECTION   Rick and Barbara Cohen

	Today	10 years	20 years	30 years
Rick's age	60	70	80	90
Barbara's age	55	65	75	85

CASH FLOW

Income

Rick - Applied Spectra, Inc.	132,000	-	-	-
Barb - Cohen & Braden, CPAs	167,500	-	-	-
Rick - Stock Option Exercise	5,000,000	-	-	-
Retirement Plans	-	78,103	135,086	206,697
Other investments	-	-	25,000	85,000
Charitable Remainder Trust	-	188,983	208,754	230,595
Total	**5,299,500**	**267,086**	**368,840**	**522,292**

Expenses

R.E. taxes	18,000	20,159	27,092	36,409
Income & Social Security taxes	1,407,621	62,553	82,829	112,259
General living	128,954	145,957	193,268	261,937

Investing

Retirement plans	44,925	-	-	-
Charitable Remainder Trust	2,000,000	-	-	-
Other Investments				
Eternity Portfolio	1,700,000	38,417	65,652	111,688
Total	**5,299,500**	**267,086**	**368,841**	**522,293**

ASSETS

Home	684,000	919,239	1,235,380	1,660,248
ASI stock options	3,200,000	-	-	-
Cohen & Braden, CPAs	642,000	-	-	-
Retirement plans	1,210,000	2,190,307	2,542,598	2,291,032
Other investments	-	483,313	738,145	653,572
Charitable Remainder Trust	2,000,000	3,817,447	4,216,837	4,658,011
Total Family Portfolio	**7,736,000**	**7,410,306**	**8,732,960**	**9,262,863**

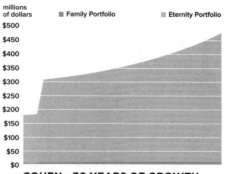

COHEN - 30 YEARS OF GROWTH

APPENDIX B
Eternity Portfolio Policy Statement

This is one family's version of an investment policy statement. While yours doesn't need to look exactly like this or be this formal, this example will give you an idea of where to start and what areas to consider.

THE JOHNSON FAMILY
ETERNITY PORTFOLIO
Investment Policy Statement
January 1, _____

I. INTRODUCTION

The purpose of this Eternity Portfolio investment policy statement is to establish a clear understanding of the goals, objectives, and management policies of the Johnson Family Eternity Portfolio ("portfolio"). The investment policy statement will:

- Serve as a written summary of our family's *current* philosophy for making eternal investments and provide a reference for future discussion.
- Create the framework for wise giving through proactive planning and documentation in the following areas:

  Determining how much to give each year (funding strategy)

  Designating broad categories for giving (asset allocation)

  Choosing the organizations to support (investment selection process)

  Keeping up with the sponsored organizations (monitoring and review)

We plan to review this investment policy statement at least annually to ensure it continues to reflect the family's God-given desires for the portfolio. Brad and Karen Johnson are the acting investment managers ("managers") of the portfolio.

II. MISSION STATEMENT

The Johnson Family Eternity Portfolio is intended to glorify God and serve His purposes by investing in strategic opportunities as described in the following statement:

> *We feel God has called us specifically to fund and be involved with ministries engaged in creative and high-yield gospel strategies with an intentional process for long-term discipling. Church-planting movements are a major part of this effort. We also desire to be involved in organizations that focus on discipling in the areas of faithful life management. Furthering the vision of Christ's church in life stewardship is a driving force within our personal mission. Brad and Karen Johnson*

Organizations of all sizes will be considered for the portfolio; however, we have a preference for opportunities to make a bigger impact in smaller organizations. That being said, we do not intend to fund more than 15 percent of any organization's annual operating budget.

The concept of leverage is important in our giving. We are actively looking for investments that demonstrate the probability of leveraged results across geographic areas, denominations, and people groups.

III. FUNDING STRATEGY

We intend to invest $35,000 cash this year in the portfolio. Current and future giving is based on, but not limited to, the exponential generosity strategy shown below.

ETERNITY PORTFOLIO
INVESTMENT SCHEDULE

INCOME	GIVING PERCENTAGE
$0-100,000	10 %
$100,001-200,000	15 %
$200,001-300,000	20 %
$300,001-up	30 %

IV. TAX POLICY

The standing policy of the portfolio is that all investments are made only to organizations exempt from U.S. income tax under section 501(c)(3) of the Internal Revenue Code. This is in keeping with a stewardship goal of minimizing income taxes. However, specific opportunities sometimes create the need to make nondeductible contributions. Direct gifts to the poor are one example of this. This tax policy is not intended to limit investments so much as it is to focus them for optimal effectiveness.

V. ASSET ALLOCATION

The following graphs show our Christian mission broken out into the three broad categories of investments for the portfolio. These categories were chosen as representative of the biblical priorities set forth in the great commandments (Matthew 22:37–39), the great commission (Matthew 28:18–20), and the overwhelming amount of Scripture on giving to the poor and needy. The main categories have been further subdivided to reflect the different subsectors of available investments.

THE CHRISTIAN MISSION ALLOCATION

The Johnson Eternity Portfolio is intended to be invested in each of the three major classes—gospel, discipleship, and mercy and justice, but with a strategic personal mission focus in church planting and Christian education.

Each of the investment organizations operates in one or more of the three phases of the Christian mission (evangelism, discipleship, mercy and justice). For example, our investment in the local church is probably equally weighted between the three.

Note that the allocation of 10 percent to the "spontaneous" category is intended to be invested as God leads in any of the other areas (local church, personal mission, poor). Historically, this has been used for one-time grants or special opportunities to minister to the poor.

The allocation of 15 percent to the poor is not our only investment in that category, as several other ministries supported within the portfolio are

JOHNSON FAMILY
ETERNITY PORTFOLIO TARGET ALLOCATION

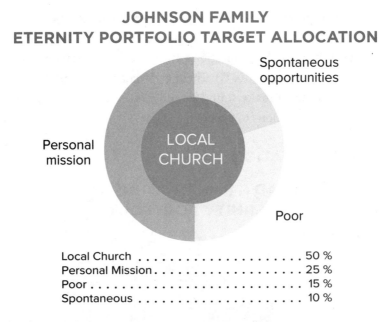

Local Church	50 %
Personal Mission	25 %
Poor	15 %
Spontaneous	10 %

actively involved in that area. However, this is the part of our portfolio where we are directly involved with the poor around us. It can consist of anonymous cash gifts to individuals, providing food or medical services, and so forth.

VI. INVESTMENT SELECTION PROCESS

Organizations are brought to our attention in any of a number of ways. Often we are introduced to ministry leaders through personal relationships. The decision of whether or not to make an investment is guided by prayer and the following process:

1. Set up an initial interview with the head of the organization (or as high up as possible).
2. Visit the site, if possible, to look at facilities and talk with personnel.
3. Review the most recent financial statements, budgets, projections, and marketing materials/proposals.
4. Network with other contacts who may know the key leaders of the organization.
5. Gain an understanding of what the organization does, how it does it, and what challenges and opportunities it faces.

During this process we are trying to answer concrete as well as intangible questions about the ministry, its leaders, its purpose, and its potential effectiveness. Some of these questions are listed in our separate due diligence checklist (see Appendix C). These criteria are not rigid but are part of the process used to make sound judgments as to which of potentially thousands of organizations to support.

VII. IMPLEMENTATION

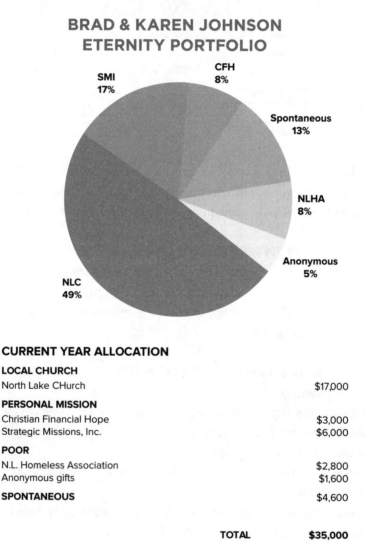

BRAD & KAREN JOHNSON ETERNITY PORTFOLIO

CURRENT YEAR ALLOCATION

LOCAL CHURCH

North Lake CHurch	$17,000

PERSONAL MISSION

Christian Financial Hope	$3,000
Strategic Missions, Inc.	$6,000

POOR

N.L. Homeless Association	$2,800
Anonymous gifts	$1,600

SPONTANEOUS

	$4,600

	TOTAL	**$35,000**

VIII. MONITORING AND REVIEW

Organizations are expected to provide regular communications regarding the status of the ministry and current developments. We review the financial and strategy updates to stay abreast of the organization's progress. If doubts arise, the investment selection process is restarted with a review of the previous answers to the due diligence checklist.

Ministries can be removed from the portfolio for a number of reasons, including the following:

- Strategy shift in the overall allocation of the portfolio
- Integrity lapses within the organization
- A pattern of inefficient use of funds
- Failure to be effective in reaching ministry objectives
- Lack of focused vision/sense of purpose
- Persistent failure to provide information on a timely basis
- Ministry not open to or ignores constructive feedback

IX. ADOPTION

We the managers of the Johnson Family Eternity Portfolio do hereby approve and adopt this investment policy statement.

Brad Johnson _____ Date _____

Karen Johnson _____ Date _____

Due Diligence Checklist

When you're considering whether to fund a specific organization, there are many issues to consider. Here's how to get started:

- Review marketing/collateral information such as the organization's website, brochures, annual report, and presentations.
- If possible, conduct a site visit or vision trip to examine the operation firsthand.
- For large gifts, meet with leadership to better understand who they are and where the organization is headed.
- Either through a face-to-face meeting, telephone call, or collateral information, try to get a sense for the following:

I. ORGANIZATIONAL ASSESSMENT

A. PURPOSE

1. What is the mission of the organization? What specifically are the major problems/issues it is trying to address?
2. What makes this organization unique?
3. What is the scope of the organization's activities (local, regional, global, country-specific)?
4. Are there well-developed, high-level goals that have been established to mark progress and give guidance to staff and donors?

B. PEOPLE

1. How well do I know the leadership? Are they visionary? Capable of leading? Passionate about the mission? Do they value relationships?
2. What qualifications do those in leadership have?
3. Does the board of directors represent a cross section of skills and qualifications needed to successfully guide an organization of this type? Are the board members investing financially in the ministry in a significant way?
4. Do the staff members understand the organization's mission and exhibit a genuine concern for their area of ministry? Do they seem content and motivated?

C. PHILOSOPHY

1. How receptive is the organization to feedback and questions? Do leaders appear transparent about problems, successes, and failures?
2. How are donors treated? Is there a demonstrated accountability for the faithful use of funds? How are volunteers recruited, trained, and utilized?
3. Does the ministry seek to create leveraged results for the kingdom (i.e., multiplication)?
4. Do there seem to be any "integrity fault lines" running through the different aspects of the ministry? Its fundraising? Programs? Communications?

D. PROCESS

1. Is there a written strategic plan for the ministry?
2. As it carries out its mission, how is the organization perceived within the community?
3. What are some of the new initiatives or activities the organization is undertaking?
4. Where does the financial support come from—a small group of major donors or a broad audience?
5. Are there audited financial statements?
6. Does the organization appear to be staffed appropriately to execute the mission?

E. PERFORMANCE

1. How does the organization measure its progress toward accomplishing the mission? Are there specific targets and objectives for the leadership as well as staff within the organization?
2. Does the organization communicate regularly and effectively with the donors? What is the frequency?
3. Is the organization accomplishing its mission?

II. PROJECT ASSESSMENT

These questions apply if a specific project is being considered for funding. Review the project proposal.

A. ORGANIZATIONAL FIT

1. Does this particular project address one of the core objectives of the

ministry? In other words, is it part of a focused, concentrated effort toward accomplishing the organization's purpose, or does it go outside of core competencies and mission?

2. Is this project or activity already being conducted successfully by another organization, and if so, are there reasons to duplicate?

3. How much of the funding is already committed?

B. PROJECT REVIEW

1. Is this a one-time investment for a project that will become a self-sustaining activity?

2. Other than in the area of funding, where are the faith hurdles? In other words, where must God supernaturally create the results for the project to be successful?

3. Do the financial projections seem reasonable? Are they too optimistic? Do they leave anything out? Is there a plan for contingencies?

4. Are there specific, measurable objectives to be accomplished?

5. How will progress be reported?

III. FINAL ASSESSMENT

1. Have I (we) spent sufficient time seeking God's will through prayer, Bible study, and wise counsel? Do I (we) have any wrong motives or conflicts of interest that should prevent this investment?

2. Assuming all indications are positive, are there any nagging questions or concerns that should be resolved?

3. How do I feel about the organization's overall approach to fundraising? Is it currently or growing toward becoming a natural process of vision casting, strategic operations, accountability and reporting to financial partners? Or is it more of a fire-drill when a new project hits the radar or financial resources start to run low? Does leadership treat the donor base as a necessary nuisance (to be patronized, wined-and-dined, etc.) or as a God-given resource (to be cultivated and included as part of the ministry team)?

4. Whether or not this appears to be a great opportunity, do I (we) feel specifically led to be involved at this time?

APPENDIX D

Resources

New organizations, books, blogs and resources of every kind continue to emerge in the generosity space. We've made no attempt to list them, but would like to highlight several unique organizations run by individuals who have been working prominently in Christian philanthropy for decades.

GENEROUSGIVING

We Are Committed to Spreading the Biblical Message of Generosity

We are like-minded peers who share your passion to wisely steward resources for God and His Kingdom.

Founded in 2000 by The Maclellan Foundation, Generous Giving's mission is to spread the biblical message of generosity in order to grow generous givers among those entrusted with much. It was launched with a vision to stir a renewed, spirit-led commitment to generosity among followers of Christ through conversation. These conversations consistently allow us and our friends to discover joy in ways we didn't expect.

Our commitment is to provide safe, solicitation-free environments. We never seek donations, permit solicitation at our events, or award grants.

What We Do

Celebration of Generosity: Generous Giving hosts a Celebration of Generosity once per year. This two-day experience brings together people entrusted with much from around the country to experience the joy of generosity and excel even more in the grace of giving. Usually 400 or more people attend this conference to be encouraged by teachings, stories, worship, and peer-to-peer interaction.

Journey of Generosity: These invite-only retreats are 24-hour gatherings hosted by an individual, couple, or organization. A trained facilitator, provided by Generous Giving free of charge, leads a small group in a deeper exploration of the life-changing message of generosity. The intimate setting encourages discussion around stories and scripture.

We will never ask you for money.	It's about conversation.	It's worth your time.
We create a safe place to talk about the abundance of generosity.	*We never tell you how or where to give.*	*Honest conversations about generosity with our peers are rare but valuable.*

APPENDIX E
Historical Quotes on Eternal Rewards

Christian leaders down through the ages have recognized the centrality of giving and eternal rewards as part of personal discipleship. Let these quotations lead you to further study.

Even if we persuade only a few, we shall obtain very great rewards, for, like good laborers, we shall receive recompense from the Master. *Justin Martyr*

Now when Christ says: make to yourselves friends, lay up for yourselves treasures, and the like, you see that he means: do good, and it will follow of itself without your seeking, that you will have friends, find treasures in heaven, and receive a reward. *Martin Luther*

God will reward every one according to his works. But this is well consistent with his distributing advantages and opportunities of improvement, according to his own good pleasure. *John Wesley*

Therefore, we should seek from none other than the Lord God whatever it is that we hope to do well, or hope to obtain as reward for our good works. *Augustine*

There are degrees of reward that are given in heaven. I'm surprised that this answer surprises so many people. I think there's a reason Christians are shocked when I say there are various levels of heaven as well as graduations of severity of punishment in hell. *R. C. Sproul*

Nothing is clearer than that a reward is promised to good works, in order to support the weakness of our flesh by some comfort; but not to inflate our minds with vain glory. *John Calvin*

The primary purpose of the Judgment Seat of Christ is the examination of the lives and service of believers, and the rewarding of them for what God considers worthy of recognition. *Theodore H. Epp*

One of the great doctrines of Christianity is our firm belief in a heavenly home. Ultimately, we shall spend eternity with God in the place He has prepared for us. And part of that exciting anticipation is His promise to reward His servants for a job well done. I don't know many believers in Jesus Christ who never think of being with their Lord in heaven, receiving His smile of acceptance, and hearing His "Well done, good and faithful servant." We even refer to one who died this way: "He has gone home to his reward." *Charles R. Swindoll*

There are many mansions in God's house because heaven is intended for various degrees of honor and blessedness. Some are designed to sit in higher places there than others; some are designed to be advanced to higher degrees of honor and glory than others are; and, therefore, there are various mansions, and some more honorable mansions and seats, in heaven than others. Though they are all seats of exceeding honor and blessedness yet some more so than others. *Jonathan Edwards*

Seek secrecy for your good deeds. Do not even see your own virtue. Hide from yourself that which you yourself have done that is commendable; for the proud contemplation of your own generosity may tarnish all your alms. Keep the thing so secret that even you yourself are hardly aware that you are doing anything at all praiseworthy. Let God be present and you will have enough of an audience. He will reward you, reward you "openly," reward you as a Father rewards a child, reward you as one who saw what you did, and knew that you did it wholly unto him. *Charles H. Spurgeon*

There will be varying degrees of reward in heaven. That shouldn't surprise us: There are varying degrees of giftedness even here on earth. *John MacArthur, Jr.*

But if it was recorded that my Jesus was received up into glory, I perceive the divine arrangement in such an act, viz., because God, who brought this to pass, commends in this way the Teacher to those who witnessed it, in order that as men who are contending not for human doctrine, but for divine teaching, they may devote themselves as far as possible to the God who is over all, and may do all things in order to please Him, as those who are to receive in the diving judgment the reward of the good or evil which they have wrought in this life. *Origen*

He is waiting to welcome us. To those who serve, to those who stand where Jesus Christ once stood many, many years ago, He promises a reward. And we can be sure He will keep His promise. *Charles R. Swindoll*

Of those who had happily finished their course, such multitudes are afterwards described, and still higher degrees of glory which they attain after a sharp fight and magnificent victory, Rev. 14:1; 15:2; 19:1; 20:4. There is an inconceivable variety in the degrees of reward in the other world. Let not any slothful one say, "If I get to heaven at all, I will be content!" Such a one may let heaven go altogether. In worldly things, men are ambitious to get as high as they can. Christians have a far more noble ambition. The difference between the very highest and the lowest state in the world is nothing in the smallest difference between the degrees of glory. *John Wesley*

And you know that, of all truths, this is the truest, that the good and godly shall obtain the good reward inasmuch as they held goodness in high esteem, which, on the other hand, the wicked shall receive meet punishment. *Clement of Alexandria*

If we are Christ's, we are here to shine for Him: by and by He will call us home to our reward. *Dwight L. Moody*

Conversely, when we see the righteous brought into affliction by the ungodly, assailed with injuries, overwhelmed with calumnies, and lacerated by insult and contumely, while, on the contrary, the wicked flourish, prosper, acquire case and honor, and all these with impunity, we ought forthwith to infer that there will be a future life in which iniquity shall receive its punishment, and righteousness its reward. *John Calvin*

Saint Augustine said that it's only by the grace of God that we ever do any-thing even approximating a good work, and none of our works are good enough to demand that God reward them. The fact that God has decided to grant rewards on the basis of obedience or disobedience is what Augus-tine called God's crowning his own works within us. If a person has been faithful in many things through many years, then he will be acknowledged by His Master, who will say to him, "Well done, thou good and faithful servant." The one who squeaks in at the last minute has precious little good works for which he can expect reward. *R. C. Sproul*

God is eager to reward us and does everything possible to help us lay up rewards. But if we are slothful and carnal, so that our service counts for nothing, we shall be saved, yet so as by fire. Let us determine by the grace of God not to be empty handed when we stand before the bema, the Judgment Seat of Christ. *Theodore H. Epp*

Therefore, he who does good works and guards himself against sin, God will reward. *Martin Luther*

If there lurks in most modern minds the notion that to desire our own good and earnestly to hope for the enjoyment of it is a bad thing, I submit that this notion has crept in from Kant and the Stoics and is not part of the Christian faith. Indeed, if we consider the unblushing promises of reward and the stag-gering nature of the rewards promised in the Gospels, it would seem that Our Lord finds our desires not too strong, but too weak. *C. S. Lewis*

For a man cannot profit God. Happy is he who judges himself an unprofit-able servant; miserable is he whom God pronounces such. But though we are unprofitable to him, our serving him is not unprofitable to us; for he is pleased to give by his grace a value to our good works which, in conse-quence of his promise, entitles us to an eternal reward. *John Wesley*

Thus Paul enjoins servants, faithfully doing what is of their duty, to hope for recompense from the Lord, but he adds "of the inheritance" (Colossians 3:24). *John Calvin*

I'd say there are at least twenty-five occasions where the New Testament clearly teaches that we will be granted rewards according to our works. Jesus frequently holds out the reward motif as the carrot in front of the horse—"great will be your reward in heaven" if you do this or that. We are called to work, to store up treasures for ourselves in heaven, even as the wicked, as Paul tells us in Romans, "treasure up wrath against the day of wrath." *R. C. Sproul*

On top of these temporal benefits connected to serving, there are eternal rewards as well. Christ Himself, while preparing the Twelve for a lifetime of serving others, promised an eternal reward even for holding out a cup of cool water. *Charles R. Swindoll*

The believer has his foundation in Jesus Christ. Now we are to build upon this foundation, and the work we have done must stand the ultimate test; final exams come at the Judgment Seat of Christ when we receive our rewards. *Billy Graham*

The kingdom of God will not be the same for all believers. Let me put it another way. Some believers will have rewards for their earthly faithfulness; other will not. Some will reign with Christ; others will not (see 2 Timothy 2:12). Some will be rich in the kingdom of God; others will be poor (see Luke 12:21, 33). Some will be given true riches; other will not (see Luke 16:11). Some will be given heavenly treasures of their own; others will not (see Luke 16:12). *Charles Stanley*

If we believe heaven to be our country, it is better for us to transmit our wealth thither, than to retain it here, where we may lose it by a sudden removal. *John Calvin*

I judge all things only by the price they shall gain in eternity. *John Wesley*

In all my years of service to my Lord, I have discovered the truth that has never failed and has never been compromised. That truth is that it is beyond the realm of possibilities that one has the ability to outgive God. Even if I give the whole of my worth to Him, He will find a way to give back to me much more than I gave. *Charles H. Spurgeon*

Looking for the reward of good works, we must wait patiently till the last day, the day of resurrection." *John Calvin*

The Lord almost always places the reward of labors and the crown of victory in heaven. *John Calvin*

I judge all things only by the price they shall gain in eternity. *John Wesley*

Any temporal possession can be turned into everlasting wealth. Whatever is given to Christ is immediately touched with immortality. *A. W. Tozer*

ABOUT THE AUTHOR

Alan Gotthardt is a nationally recognized investment advisor who has spent nearly three decades focused on the intersection of faith and money. As an author, advisor and speaker, he has helped thousands of families across the income spectrum manage their money for lasting results.

Alan is Managing Director and Chief Investment Officer at TriniD Capital, a private investment company. Formerly the President of Brightworth, Alan was part of the leadership team that built the company into a nationally recognized wealth management firm. He has been listed in Robb Report Worth magazine as one of the Nation's 100 Most Exclusive Wealth Advisors.

Alan earned undergraduate and graduate business degrees at the University of Georgia. He also completed the IMCA Investment Analyst Program at the Wharton School and is a Certified Investment Management Analyst[SM] as well as a Certified Public Accountant. Alan serves a number of nonprofit organizations on a volunteer basis. He and his wife, Melissa, have three children.

Connect with Alan:
Web: EternityPortfolio.com
Facebook: Facebook.com/EternityPortfolio

GUEST CONTRIBUTORS

David Wills
President, National Christian Foundation

David is president of National Christian Foundation (NCF), a position he has held since 1998. Under his leadership, NCF has become the world's largest Christian grant-making foundation, serving more than 12,000 families. Historically, NCF has distributed more than $4.5 billion in grants to more than 30,000 charitable organizations all over the world. David has co-authored two books, *Investing in God's Business* and *Family.Money,* as well as numerous articles. David serves on several boards, including the Evangelical Council for Financial Accountability (ECFA), ProVision Foundation, Global Generosity Foundation, Chick-fil-A Foundation, and Generous Giving, of which he is cofounder. David and his wife, Chris, live near Atlanta with their seven children.

Dr. Johnny Hunt
Senior Pastor, First Baptist Church Woodstock

Dr. Johnny Hunt is senior pastor of the 19,000-member First Baptist Church, Woodstock, Georgia. He was the previous president of the Southern Baptist Convention and with his wife of forty-four years, Janet, is the founder of Timothy+Barnabas, a ministry of teaching and encouraging pastors and their wives. An author of numerous books, including *Building Your Leadership Resume* and *Shoe Leather Christianity*, Dr. Hunt also serves on the board of numerous organizations. He has been involved in strategic giving since his first days as a Christian. Johnny and Janet live in Woodstock, Georgia, where they enjoy their two daughters and four grandchildren.

Todd Harper
President, Generous Giving

Todd Harper, one of the founders of Generous Giving, has been actively engaged in spreading the biblical message of generosity for more than ten years. In his role as president, Todd acts as the key spokesperson for Generous Giving, managing relationships with givers and implementing strategies for advancing the generosity message. He holds a BA in economics and entrepreneurship from Baylor University and previously served for eleven years with Campus Crusade for Christ International in Russia, Yugoslavia, and in the United States. Prior to joining Generous Giving, Todd was a partner in an investment management firm, advising high net worth clients on growing and using wealth wisely. Todd is passionate about discipling others and, specifically, encouraging Christians to excel in the grace of giving. He and his wife, Collynn, and their five children live in Orlando, Florida.

Larry Powell
President, Powell Family Enterprises, LLC
Larry manages Powell Family Enterprises, LLC, a private equity investment company in Atlanta. Previously he served as president of Powell & Company Insurance from 1978 to 1991, before it sold to AON Risk Services, Inc., of Georgia, a subsidiary of AON. Powell has invested in and served on the boards of a number of private companies. He currently serves on the board of Generous Giving and as a trustee of the Maclellan Foundation, In addition, he serves on the boards of Family Christian Ministries, My House Ministries, and FaithBridge Foster Care, and on the Stewardship Team at North Point Community Church. He received a BBA from the University of Georgia (Magna Cum Laude) and a Masters of Insurance from Georgia State University. Larry and his wife, Betsy, reside in Atlanta.

Heather Tuininga
Marigold Associates
Heather Tuininga oversees philanthropic advising services for Marigold Associates. She relishes helping people, families, and organizations strategically align their giving to achieve the impact and outcomes they envision. Her roles have included executive director of a private family foundation, philanthropic advisor, program officer at the Bill & Melinda Gates Foundation, and fiscal

analyst for the Washington state legislature. A native of Washington state, Heather holds an MA in Public Policy from Duke University and a BA in Political Science and Economics from Central Washington University, where she was a Presidential Scholar.

Heather is committed to strategic philanthropy and helping people "move the needle" on issues they care about while experiencing the joy of giving. In addition to teaching seminars on generosity and finance, Heather provides volunteer financial coaching for families in need. She serves on the finance committee at her church and on the boards of African Leadership and Reconciliation Ministries and the National Christian Foundation— Seattle. Heather and her husband live in Issaquah, Washington.

Lorne Jackson, CFP, CLU, CH.F.C.
President, Canadian National Christian Foundation
After twenty-five years in the financial services business, Lorne sold his company and left the "for profit" world in 2002 to create the Canadian National Christian Foundation (CNCF) as a federally incorporated public foundation to serve donors in Canada wanting to give more efficiently and with more flexibility. Lorne works with Christian financial advisors and charity leaders in funding God's work across Canada and around the world. With a passion for giving and overall stewardship, Lorne has written *After the Faith Decision . . . All Else Is Stewardship*, reminding readers that stewardship is about all of life as we live for our Lord. Lorne and Doris have been married forty-five years and have two married children and four grandchildren.

Jack Alexander
The ReImagine Group
With a passion for Christ's kingdom, Jack has cofounded and built business services and technology companies ranging from 5 to 6,000 employees. He has spent the last twelve years serving as a coach, advisor, and board member to several ministries and businesses as well as speaking regularly to ministries and churches. Currently, he runs The ReImagine Group, an organization that creates resources to come alongside churches to build cultures

of generosity. Over the years, Jack has received numerous awards, including Ernst & Young's National Entrepreneur of the Year Award for Principle-Centered Leadership, *Business Travel News*'s Top 25 most-influential executives, and the Family Honors Award by the Georgia Center for Opportunity. He and Lisa have three grown sons and three grandsons.

Sharon Epps
Co-Founder, Women Doing Well
Sharon is a strategic and discerning leader, serving as co-founder of Women Doing Well and as a member of the management team of Generous Church. She has a background in corporate banking, as a stewardship pastor and as an executive with Crown Financial Ministries. As a speaker and consultant, Sharon's passion is helping churches and individuals experience the joy and freedom of generosity. Sharon lives in Buford, Georgia, with her husband and a revolving door of family and friends.

Charlie Jordan
Partner, Brightworth
Charlie is a partner and wealth advisor at Brightworth focusing on integrating wealth planning, tax and estate planning, investment management, and philanthropic counsel into a customized strategy to help clients accomplish their life and financial goals. In addition to advanced charitable planning expertise acquired as a manager at the National Christian Foundation, Charlie is a CERTIFIED FINANCIAL PLANNER™ practitioner and received his Master of Accountancy with a concentration in taxation from Kennesaw State University. He graduated from the University of Florida with an undergraduate degree in finance. Charlie currently serves on the boards of the Georgia Planned Giving Council and the Fellowship of Christian Athletes East Cobb, and is an inaugural member of the Children's Healthcare of Atlanta Legacy Advisory Council. Charlie and his wife, Krysta, have three daughters.

NOTES

Foreword

1. Howard Marks, with Davis, Greenblatt, Johnson, and Klarman, *The Most Important Thing, Illuminated: Uncommon Sense for the Thoughtful Investor* (New York: Columbia University Press, 2011).

Introduction

1. www.GlobalRichList.com.

Chapter 1: Faithful Managers

1. John F. MacArthur, Jr., *The MacArthur New Testament Commentary on Matthew 1–7* (Chicago: Moody Publishers, 1985), 425.
2. Erwin Lutzer, *Your Eternal Reward* (Chicago: Moody Publishers, 1998), 38.
3. As quoted in Douglas M. Lawson, *Give to Live* (La Jolla, CA: ALTI Publications, 1991), 81.

Chapter 2: The Ultimate Investment

1. Lutzer, 21.
2. Thomas Gouge, *Riches Increased by Giving* (Harrisonburg, VA: Sprinkle Publications, 1992), 44.
3. Randy Alcorn, *In Light of Eternity* (Colorado Springs: WaterBrook Press, 1999), 125.
4. John F. MacArthur, Jr., *The MacArthur New Testament Commentary on 1 Timothy* (Chicago: Moody Publishers, 1985), 285.
5. Jonathan Edwards, *Heaven—A World of Love* (Amityville, NY: Calvary Press Publishing, 1999), 57.

Chapter 3: The Eternity Portfolio

1. John F. MacArthur, Jr., *The MacArthur New Testament Commentary on Matthew 1–7* (Chicago: Moody Publishers, 1985), 411.
2. Samuel Harris, *The Scriptural Plan of Benevolence* (New York: American Tract Society, circa 1850), 25.

3. Parsons Cooke, *The Divine Law of Beneficence* (New York: American Tract Society, circa 1850), 43.
4. Margaret Thatcher, Speech to the General Assembly to the Church of Scotland, May 21, 1988, www.margaretthatcher.org.

Chapter 4: Funding the Portfolio: How Much Is Enough for Now?

1. Harris, 11.
2. Assuming no adjusted gross income (AGI) limitation on itemized deductions.

Chapter 6: God's Asset Allocation

1. Andrew Carnegie, *The Gospel of Wealth* (Bedford, MA: Applewood Books, 1998), 15.
2. "Directions in Women's Giving," Women Doing Well. http://www.womendoingwell.org/index.php/resources, 2012.
3. "Financial Experience and Behaviors Among Women," Prudential Research Study, 2011.
4. Sharon Epps, "Bringing Women into the Eternity Portfolio Conversation," 2014.
5. Sharon Epps, "Women: The Kingdom Needs Your Voice," 2014.
6. Ibid.
7. Cooke, 79.
8. Ibid., 80.

Chapter 7: Making Wise Investments

1. Bill Bright, *How You Can Experience the Adventure of Giving* (Orlando, FL: New Life Publications, 2002), 19.
2. Ibid., 20.
3. Richard Steckel and Jennifer Lehman, *In Search of America's Best Nonprofits* (San Francisco: Jossey-Bass Publishers, 1997), 54.
4. Gary Miller and Nathan Wright, *The Other Side of the Wall* (Berlin, OH: TGS International, 2013) 167.
5. Robert Lupton, *Toxic Charity* (New York: HarperCollins, 2012), 7.

6. Steve Corbett and Brian Fikkert, *When Helping Hurts: Alleviating Poverty without Hurting the Poor and Yourself* (Chicago: Moody Publishers, 2009) 52.

7. Ibid., 59.

8. Ibid., 52.

9. Lupton, 12, 238.

10. Miller, 160.

11. Ibid. See also Corbett and Fikkert, 99 and 101: "A helpful first step in thinking about working with the poor in any context is to discern whether the situation calls for relief, rehabilitation, or development. In fact, the failure to distinguish among these situations is one of the most common reasons that poverty-alleviation efforts often do harm. . . . One of the biggest mistakes that North American churches make—by far—is in applying relief in situations in which rehabilitation or development is the appropriate intervention."

12. Miller, 171.

13. Ibid.

14. Corbett, 90.

15. Miller, 29.

16. Corbett, 65.

17. Miller, 171.

18. Ibid.

19. Lupton, 9.

20. Miller, 102.

21. Lupton, 161.

22. Corbett, 61.

23. Lupton, 9.

24. Lupton, 81.

Chapter 8: Passing the Baton

1. I am grateful to Howard Dayton and Larry Burkett for helping shape some of my thoughts on teaching financial principles to children.

2. Andrew Carnegie, American industrialist and philanthropist (1835-1919).

Chapter 9: The Seven Golden Keys to Investing for Eternity

1. Bill Bright, *The Christian and Giving (Ten Basic Steps toward Christian Maturity, Step 8)* (Orlando, FL: New Life Publications, 2002), 17.
2. George Barna, *How to Increase Giving in Your Church* (Ventura, CA: Regal Books, 1997), 50.